Irish Bitches
Be Crazy

D0522923

Emma Comerford

NEW ISLAND

IRISH BITCHES BE CRAZY

First published in 2015 by
New Island Books
16 Priory Hall Office Park
Stillorgan
County Dublin
Republic of Ireland

www.newisland.ie

PRINT ISBN: 978-1-84840-481-6
EPUB ISBN: 978-1-84840-482-3
MOBI ISBN: 978-1-84840-483-0

British Library Cataloguing Data.
A CIP catalogue record for this book is available from the British Library.

Typeset by JVR Creative India
Cover design by Anna Morrison
Printed by ScandBook AB, Sweden

10 9 8 7 6 5 4 3 2 1

In loving memory of Sarah Monahan, a beautiful Irish woman who, by her very nature, disproved my hypothesis.

Contents

Introduction

There is a stereotypical Irish woman that exists in the minds of many. She is oftentimes a Mammy and typically displays the following characteristics: talkative, bossy, jovial, quick-tempered, God-fearing and heavy-drinking. The use of stereotypes is generally considered to be misguided as it often leads to bias. As a nation, the Irish are no strangers to bias and the subsequent discrimination that it generates. Being both Irish and female myself, I decided to embark on a journey of discovery to unearth the true nature of an Irish woman. Following careful analysis, I found that most of the traits attributed to Irish females are, in fact, true. Rather than debunking the myths, I have extended them. Each of the following chapters delves into the essence of an Irish woman, expounding many of the old chestnuts and proposing some new theories.

This pigeonholing is not confined to an Irish woman's personality traits and can also be applied to an Irish woman's appearance. What mental image springs to mind when people talk about women from Ireland? Is she represented as a Celtic waif with delicate pale skin and flowing red tresses? Perhaps it is the symbolic earth mother, equipped with massive nurturing breasts and childbearing hips? Is it fuck.

What people the world over envision is a snipey Mrs Doyle type who is small of stature with a narrow face and mousy brown hair. She wears a heavy woollen coat and ugly shoes. Additionally, this generic Irish woman is a heavy drinker who loves to gossip, would sell her firstborn for a bargain and whose capacity for profanity would make a biker blush.

Could these universally held perceptions be correct, and, if so, how did we become like this? What perverse combination of nature and nurture moulded us into this fascinating creature? As a self-appointed agent for Irish women the world over, I attempt to explore the influences of biological and environmental factors that shape an Irish woman's personality. Complex psychological and sociological issues will be examined, ranging from an Irish woman's inability to accept compliments to her approach to the book club phenomenon, as well as looking at a number of key indicators, such as how Irish women behave at funerals and their uncomfortable relationship with sex. Many sections contain helpful 'How to' guides, which ignore the more traditional cookery and domestic goddess tips and proffer advice to today's Irish woman on such matters as The Dignified Walk of Shame, and Being Sworn to Secrecy (exactly how many people can you tell?) The book pays special attention to the role played by Catholic propaganda and alcohol in shaping this embodiment of Celtic femininity.

Many Irish women are leading a double life, torn between the old traditional role of an Irish woman and the demands of modern-day society. On the one hand, the female population of Ireland is highly educated and career-driven, yet on the other hand many still attend Mass on a regular basis. Indeed, a recent study on dual-worker households in this country concluded that Irish women are still doing three-quarters of the housework. Furthermore, once their daily professional and domestic duties have been dealt with, they are no longer seeking solace in the form of a nice cup of tea. The new wine culture in Ireland is playing a pivotal role in influencing the drinking habits of the middle-aged Irish female as they are increasingly turning to the grape and consuming wine at home. In tandem, 16% of young Irish women are binge drinking on a weekly basis. Twice as many fights and accidents occur amongst Irish female drinkers than in other countries. All of this brings into question, are they saints, scholars or Cillit Bang™-wielding winos – what does it really mean to be a present-day Irish woman?

Following extensive research, the genesis of this dichotomy became apparent. The journey from Peig Sayers to Miriam O'Callaghan has been arduous for the Irish woman; the struggle to find expression in a patriarchal society, to escape the dominance of the Catholic Church and to control a tendency towards alcohol abuse and other manifestations of low self-esteem. The end result of this pilgrimage is a nation filled with functioning female lunatics. This may come as a surprise as their underlying madness is not immediately apparent. However, once you scratch the surface you will find beneath it a teeming mass of neuroses. This alarming situation is often overlooked as Irish women are also found to be amusing and compassionate, and will frequently distract the casual observer by pumping them full of tea and/or wine before dulling their senses with small talk about the price of houses.

Irish Bitches Be Crazy expounds this theory and offers helpful instructions on the safest way to interact with these erratic yet charismatic individuals.

1.
Virgin Monologues

The first thing you need to understand about Irish women is that they are deeply religious beings. Whether they admit it or not, all Irish women know the lyrics of every hymn ever written and the words of all known prayers. In keeping with the most effective propaganda techniques, they were drummed into them as part of the Irish school syllabus. Consequently, the regurgitation of any prayer results in the achievement of a trance-like state and the spewing forth of words in a rapid and unintelligible manner that sounds like an old-fashioned cassette tape in fast-forward mode.

⚡ Coveting ⚡

Most Irish women's beliefs are rooted in the jealous and vengeful God of the Old Testament. Not for them the wishy-washy 'New Age' God that emerged in the New Testament. They like their religious idols to partake in a bit of smiting, and they take their religion with a large side order of superstition. They believe in God and the afterlife, angels and the devil, in the same way that they believe in fairies, ghosts and not walking under ladders. Additionally, all Irish women were born saddled with Original Sin. They are constantly playing catch-up and trying to please a God and a Church, both of which have already condemned their souls to eternal damnation as a default starting point. In keeping with the French judicial system, we are guilty until proven otherwise. No matter how many Hail Marys and Our Fathers an Irish woman utters in her lifetime, or how many virtual goats she sends to the developing world, she is more than likely going straight to hell. The main offence committed by these paragons of virtue is the coveting of their neighbour's goods. They are unashamed, unrepentant coveters. They live and breathe covetous thoughts. They covet their neighbour's car, her tarmacadamed drive, the number of days' annual leave she gets and her sickeningly perfect overachieving children. They don't do sloth, can take or leave adultery, but they tend to crumble when it comes to a bit of coveting. They have also been known to taketh the Lord's name in vain after a couple of Pinot Grigios.

⚡ Irish Karma ⚡

Irish women don't believe in the random nature of the universe. Everything happens for a reason, and what goes around comes around. If you perform a dastardly deed, you *will* get your comeuppance. In Ireland, when someone behaves badly and profits from their actions, it is widely agreed that they will have no luck from it. A false insurance claim will precede falling down the stairs. Ripping someone off is a sure way to bring on a hernia. Being Irish and innately 'cute hoors' they have devised a way of nullifying the negative effect of Irish Karma: all you have to do is donate twenty euro to the St Vincent de Paul to take the bad luck out of it, problem solved. They have a strong belief system that is not always limited to the confines of the Catholic church. The more you get to know an Irish woman the more her witchy tendencies emerge. Your common or garden religions don't interest her. Her God is of the vindictive, all-powerful, all-seeing and all-knowing variety. She dances at the crossroads, howls at the moon, then puts on her Sunday best and heads off to Mass in the morning. So, be warned, this is not a woman to cross. She has a variety of different methods for dealing with her adversaries.

⋏ Witchy Practices ⋏

Many of these Irish women are going about their daily lives working in Accounts Payable and coming home to their husbands of forty years. However, unbeknownst to anyone, they are secretly engaged in nocturnal foraging for toxic plants and spitting into poultices for the production of a curse or kibosh. Its purpose? The destruction of the new Financial Software System being implemented in their department at work. Once the concoction has been made, they make the sign of the cross over it to keep on the good side of their Heavenly Father, then unleash it on the unsuspecting software tool. Failing that, they resort to a verbal onslaught on the software consultancy team in the form of some quaint old Irish invocations. They utilise the following 'widow's curses', listed in order of increasing evilness:

* *Mallacht Dé ort* = God's curse on you.

* *Cac muice ar do shúil* = Pig shit in your eye.

* *Mo chuid tubaiste ort* = May you have my bad luck as well.

* *Go mbuaile an bhuinneach thú* = May you be stricken with diarrhoea.

* *Nach raibh tú beo ar maidin* = May you be dead by the morning.

Civil servant by day and *cailleach* or crone by night, these women may be clean-living and God-fearing but they have a deeply ingrained madness that emerges whenever the Lord isn't taking their calls and they have to take matters into their own hands.

⚡ Mickey Dodgers ⚡

The Catholic Church was an authoritative institution for many years in Ireland. Priests and nuns had the same jurisdiction and power as the gardaí and represented a type of moral law enforcement. Nuns ran the educational institutions for females, and therefore had a huge influence on the lives of Irish women. Ultimately, they spent their formative years in the company of these 'mickey dodgers'. As a result, even the most secular Irish woman will bless themselves when a funeral cortège drives past and perform a self-conscious bobbing genuflection upon entering a church. Also, just because she fled Ireland to live in a yurt in the Sudanese desert, don't think for one moment that she would be happy with anything other than a full church wedding with 300 guests and having her children attain the entire range of sacraments on offer during the course of their lives.

Young Irish girls received their first introduction to nuns in primary school, where the lay teachers brainwashed them into believing that all nuns were kind, angelic beings. The teachers read stories to the juniors about successful 'career nuns' who had managed to attain sainthood. The books contained illustrations depicting the saints as beautiful young girls surrounded by adoring children with a couple of rabbits or lambs in attendance, and maybe a robin perched on one shoulder, like a Disney still. The reality was a tad different.

So much so, in fact, that if you even say the word 'nun' in front of an Irish woman today they flinch involuntarily and then shudder at the horrific memories the word invokes.

Here's a telling questionnaire for the Irish female populace. It is posed *Cosmo* style:

Imagine that you are in a lift. The doors open. A nun enters and glances in your direction. Do you:

    a) Smile respectfully then quietly utter 'Hello, Sister' with a very slight bobbing motion indicative of a curtsey?

b) Break into a cold sweat, hyperventilate, then visualise raising an ancient samurai sword over your head to impale the bitch?

c) Ignore her, just in case the whole celibacy thing is in some way contagious?

If you chose answer (a) or (b) then you are an Irish woman who has suffered years of systematic abuse while being educated by nuns. If, however, you chose answer (c), I am afraid you are probably a filthy whore and most definitely a Protestant.

⚔ Celebrity Nuns ⚔

A popular misconception about nuns is that they have been around since the dark ages – and some of the nuns that you have encountered may look like they were actually born around that time. However, the first Orders only emerged during the fifteenth century following authorisation from the Pope of the time. Another common theory is that women only choose to become nuns out of desperation or to prevent death by starvation. In fact, the first nuns in Europe were women from wealthy families. There were a number of reasons why they decided to reject the traditional

11

female role of wifey in favour of marriage to a more heavenly groom. Very often they didn't want to marry some minger who had been chosen for them by their parents. Perhaps the girls just got bored of playing the piano and painting watercolours all day so decided to adopt an altruistic philosophy of helping the sick, the elderly and the poor. It is equally plausible that some of these women were gay and sought refuge from a homophobic society that condemned the love that dare not speak its name. Or sometimes their fathers would simply baulk at paying out a huge dowry and forced their daughters into a convent to save money.

St Bridget

St Bridget was the inaugural celebrity nun, and is credited with rounding up the first posse of nuns in Ireland. She was primarily a pagan goddess who the Christians decided to take all the credit for – just like they did with Christmas and Easter. She was rumoured to be our first lesbian saint. Irrespective of which team she was batting for, she was considered to be a very spiritual lady and performed many miracles in her day.

Most of these supernatural occurrences were food related; she was like the Nigella Lawson of the nun world but without the blow job impersonations. One such miracle occurred when she had given away all her mother's butter to a beggar and the butter dish was miraculously replenished. This singular act was said to inspire the Super Size Me phenomenon that emerged in later years. Legend has it that Bridget performed a healing miracle as a result of a horse riding accident. Apparently, she fell off her horse and hit her head on a stone. The blood she lost was mixed with water and poured onto the heads of mute siblings, who were then able to talk. This miracle was possibly the precursor to the Blarney Stone myth. If ever there was a superfluous Irish custom, it is the practice of kissing the Blarney Stone and thereafter being endowed with the gift of the gab. It is akin to the Germans having a superstitious practice that transforms them into control freaks.

Whenever Irish girls were being force-fed these pointless stories as part of their 'education', it gave rise to the universal juvenile opinion that the saint was shamefully wasting her remarkable holy powers. Might she not have done something a bit more worthwhile, like ejecting the English from the country or providing the Irish peasantry with a lifetime supply of Cup-a-Soup?

Despite the aforementioned amazing talents, Bridget is mostly remembered for making a cross out of straw. Ironically, although she is celebrated for her generosity to poor people, she was responsible for putting Kildare on the map; an enclave near Dublin where they have replaced Christianity with the worship of money and horses.

St Catherine

Another firm favourite with Irish nuns was St Catherine of Sienna. They delighted in recounting the story of how Catherine became a nun. Catherine's father was an Italian wool dyer named Giacomo di Benincasa who fathered twenty-six children (unsurprisingly, the nuns did not dwell on this particular historical detail). Giacomo was opposed to Catherine's religious leanings and argued vehemently with his daughter about her desire to become a nun. Catherine had many visions throughout her life, one of which involved Jesus placing a ring on her finger symbolising her marriage to the Church. The nuns also neglected to mention that it was no ordinary wedding band; instead of gold it was made from ... the blessed foreskin of the baby Jesus – a popular relic at the time.

The inclusion of this nugget of information would have livened up the celebrity nun story sessions by lending them a more Tarantinoesque air. The nuns could have vamped it up a little with some chainsaw-wielding fourteenth-century schoolgirls chasing Our Lord around, Lorena Bobbitt style. Instead, their most shocking pronouncement related to Catherine cutting off all her hair in an attempt to thwart her parents' desire to marry her off. Most Irish schoolgirls couldn't have been more horrified by a boy band break-up. Catherine's ploy had the desired effect: Giacomo relented and agreed to let her become a nun.

Today, St Catherine's disembodied head can be viewed in the Church of San Dominico in Tuscany, along with one of her thumbs. Her body is in Rome, and her foot is said to be in a reliquary in Venice. Now, that is what an Irish woman would refer to as a 'fine spread'.

Violent with Piety

Worshipping religious artifacts is alive and well in modern-day Ireland. To commemorate the 750th anniversary of the discovery of St Anthony's tongue, two of the saint's relics were brought on tour to Galway, Dublin, Wexford, Cork and Limerick. The relics themselves consisted of a piece of skin and a piece of petrified flesh. They were unceremoniously stored in a suitcase in the back of a Ford Galaxy. They were then driven from church to church by three friars. Although support for the Church in Ireland has waned in recent years, tens of thousands of people turned out to venerate the relics. Traffic ground to a halt in Galway as 30,000 people made their way to the cathedral in the centre of the city. Worshipping took on the intensity of an Irish water charges protest. Then, contrary to the camaraderie of a peaceful protest, the crowd began jostling each other in a frenzied bid for optimal viewing positions. The female devotees proved to be far more aggressive than their male counterparts, the scrambling intensified, and the Irish women became violent with piety.

The Catholic Church's worship of body parts is not considered perverse or creepy, and neither St Bridget nor St Catherine was ever deemed to have mental health issues in keeping with their protoplasmic pervsions.

Closed Orders

Early Irish nuns were probably heavily influenced by trendy French and Italian nuns who spent their days smoking Gauloises, shrugging their shoulders nonchalantly and zipping around town on trendy pink Lambrettas to visit the sick and the poor. However, the reality of visiting sick people in Ireland was that you ran the risk of contracting the bubonic plague, and so Irish nuns improvised and came up with the idea of enclosed orders such as the Poor Clares.

Closed Orders were safer as they had little or no contact with the outside world, which greatly reduced the chances of catching the Black Death. Today there are twenty-nine contemplative women's convents remaining in Ireland, and the women who enter these convents give away all their worldly possessions. They only ever leave the convent grounds to vote against abortion referendums or to play the Lotto.

The Calling

If a life of isolation, contemplation and poverty wasn't your *raison d'être*, you could always join an order that specialised in education such as the Dominican nuns, thereby dedicating your life to screaming abuse at surly teenagers.

Irish women who received their secondary education in a convent have a lasting impression of the nuns as a tribe of very angry women with overactive salivary glands – reminiscent of the Gestapo, but with more facial hair. To say that they felt no connection with them is an understatement of epic proportion.

In fact, they did not even consider the nuns to be the same species as themselves, and yet, presumably, once upon a time, they too were young girls full of their own hopes and dreams.

Then they got … the CALLING. And that was it.

They were fucked, metaphorically speaking.

Because, as we all know, once you get the CALLING you have no option but to don your sackcloth, close down your clitoral account, and away off with you to a convent *tout de suite*.

Young Irish girls lived in fear that they, too, would have their lives irreversibly ruined by receiving the CALLING. They would lie in bed at night with the covers over their head suffering from epiphany aversion, petrified that their room had become piped for Jesus, the surround sound of the Lord. Thankfully for most girls, the CALLING never came. Maybe they were just too godless and wicked, or maybe they were just too sane.

A young girl recently spoke on YouTube about her CALLING and how unexpected it was. Sister Alison received the CALLING while she was in an airport. It was an inner voice that told her she had been chosen to be 'Christ's Bride' – a concept that seems unhinged on many different levels. Firstly, it was obviously a flight announcement that she misheard – an oversight that could happen to anyone. However, it is unusual for someone to mishear a flight announcement that prompts them to give away all their worldly possessions and stop bleaching their facial hair. Secondly, the idea of a young girl who wants to be Christ's Bride strikes me as the stuff of a Neil Jordan movie, all heaving prepubescent breasts and very few decent car chases. Or maybe that's just this author....

Nun Recruitment Drives

The Dominican Order ran regular Nun Recruitment Drives, or Retreat Weekends, as they were called. All unsuspecting teenage girls were collected by the school bus and driven to a retreat centre where they spent their days in the company of a young, trendy priest. The priest would be disguised as a human being wearing a woolly jumper, jeans and sandals. He would befriend the girls by smoking cigarettes and playing the guitar. Inhumane propaganda techniques included repeatedly playing 'The Boxer' followed by the enforced singing in rounds of the torturous 'He's Got the Whole World in His Hands'. Occasionally the priest would single out one of the girls and inform them that they had Nun's Eyes. Rather than inspiring the chosen one to take the cloth, this declaration was more likely to cause her to flee to the kitchen and attempt to gouge her own eyes out with a soup spoon.

They upped the ante in secondary school, when the nuns were tasked with teaching a range of subjects including Latin and history. The fact that they had no teaching qualifications and no apparent knowledge of their chosen subjects was irrelevant. Instead, pupils mostly learned about the devastating effect that forty years of celibacy and the daily ingestion of cabbage soup can have on a woman.

The real eye-opener would occur during the monthly visit of the parish priest, when the nuns would magically transform from hysterical harridan to simpering sycophant. Their nauseating kowtowing gave the girls a wonderful insight into how women should behave in front of male authority figures in Ireland. Watching their skilled performance and paying close attention to the minute details, such as the need to paw at the priest's forearm at every given opportunity and burst into uncontrollable knee-slapping laughter when he deigned to speak, served them well in later years when applying for bank loans and dealing with punctures at the side of the road.

The worst crime you could possibly commit was 'to give back cheek' when the parish priest was in attendance. The nun was then faced with a difficult choice: she could either pretend that she hadn't heard the insolence, or perform the kind of sudden double switch of personalities that would make a seasoned schizophrenic proud. A nun could contort her face in rage and verbally attack the offender in spluttering splendour, then revert to adoration mode before you could say 'Custard Cream, Father?'

At the end of the day, the nuns were more pitied than scorned. After the bell rang and the priest had moved on to the next class the girls would file out of the classroom and watch the nun's receding back as she scurried off down the corridor. It was remininiscent of that poignant scene at the end of every *Incredible Hulk* episode when Dr Bruce Banner would emerge from the shadows with his clothes in flitters. He would turn and jog off into the distance, weary from his recent physical metamorphosis and buckled by self-righteousness.

Boarding School

The daily battle between the nuns and the schoolgirls was intense, but at least both parties had the opportunity to go home at 4 p.m., take stock and prepare for the next day's skirmishes. Some Irish girls were not so lucky as their parents saw fit to send them to convent boarding schools. The nuns who ran these board-ing schools were younger, and therefore harboured more bitterness. Their task was not an easy one: they were responsible for the care of more than a hundred pubescent teenage girls.

So, you had a slightly sinister grey institutional building, located in a remote part of Ireland, which was teeming full of demonic hormones. It is a miracle that the only blood that flowed was of the menstrual kind. The females imprisoned in one of these boarding schools would all get their period at the same time. Once a month, progesterone and oestrogen levels plummeted and kick-started the inevitable: irritability, sadness, depression, emotional sensitivity, tiredness, weepiness, and the inability to operate heavy machinery. Taking their cue from all good werewolf movies, the nuns would batten down the hatches, cancel any impending visits from the outside world, and endure the five- to seven-day onslaught of The Curse.

Ordinary day-to-day living in these schools was no picnic either, with ongoing deprivations such as eating meals in silence, being forced to clean out toilets, going to bed during daylight hours, only being allowed to wash once a week, and a savage amount of praying. Other hardships involved the nuns reading all incoming mail, listening in on phone calls and practising ritual humiliations of the girls. After lock-up the boarders would lie awake in their cubicles listening to all the other miserable Irish girls crying themselves to sleep – waterboarding was performed on Wednesdays. Meanwhile, the sisters tucked themselves up in palatial splendour, eating fresh fruit and reading the latest edition of *Gulags for Dummies*. Day school was sublime by comparison.

Then there were the rumours of lesbian nuns who were waiting to seduce any unsuspecting schoolgirl who veered off the path on her way through the convent. Rumour had it that there were certain nuns who hung out in the changing rooms and offered to assist the girls with getting changed after hockey practice. These nuns weren't adverse to a bit of white knee sock fetish. More often than not, the most overtly sexual act performed by Irish nuns was repeatedly smoothing their grey cardigans over their incarcerated breasts. In fact, the grey cardie is the inanimate object that is most likely to trigger the latent sphenisciphobia in generations of Irish women. This fear of nuns may have lain dormant for decades when suddenly they become overwhelmed by it on their way through Marks & Spencer's woollen section.

There is no doubt that the majority of Irish women have been psychologically damaged by the concept of original sin and the never-ending Catholic guilt trip that is imposed on them from an early age. It is equally true that Irish women are a section of society with an overwhelming sense of altruism and unselfishness. They rarely hesitate when it comes to giving their time, and are exceedingly generous. In fact, if you are lucky enough to have an Irish woman in your corner, she will support you and care for you with a kindness and fanaticism that is verging on creepy. Amen to the Irish woman and her Christian values.

2.
The Dead

Irish Women Love a Good Funeral

The majority of Irish women have a morbid fascination with tragedy and death. It'd be fair to say that we love a good catastrophe; the more tragic the better. This obsession may appear a little perverse to an outsider, but it is a side effect of being from a small, traditionally poor country with a peasant population. Ireland's tragic history and its tight-knit communities have ensured that death and despair are part of our national heritage.

Being a country where, historically, the population eked out a living from fishing and farming, we have had ample opportunities for grievous accidents. Subsistence living positively encourages these catastrophes. When such a calamity occurs, a man with a beard and a woolly jumper will hurry home to write a poem or a song about it. These laments usually have a minimum of twenty verses, each one more morbid and depressing than the last. The opening bars can clear a pub in seconds flat. By verse number ten, the remaining listeners have lost the will to live and would gladly leap into a nearby slurry pit to put an end to the never-ending dirge.

⋈ Distracting an Irish Woman ⋈

If you ever find yourself on the wrong side of an Irish woman, you can use her fatalistic fascination as a diversionary tactic. Distract her with stories of ill-fated orphans and people dropping dead on the day of their retirement. She will be utterly riveted by your sad tale and completely forget about you crashing her car or shifting her sister. If you can manage to make her cry with your tales of woe, she will be delighted. There is nothing an Irish woman likes more than a good old bawl, and she will never be more content than when she is watching a tragically sad tear-jerker like *P.S. I Love You*, eating a bucket of popcorn, sobbing into her Barry's Tea with a big, happy, crying head on her. A fit of crying is like a replacement orgasm, and both events are always followed by a Marlboro Light. If you see her reaching for her packet of twenty, you know it's a job well done.

⚡ Ireland's Got Torment ⚡

An Irish woman's hardships are worn like a badge of honour, and are often the subject of fierce competition. Woe betide the person who usurps their misfortunes. There are some Irish women who triumphantly proclaim that their upbringing makes *Angela's Ashes* look like a comedy. In keeping with the current era of TV talent competitions, we could cash in on this national penchant for misery and introduce some new television shows to the nation entitled *Distress Factor* or *Ireland's Got Torment*.

These shows would follow the standard format, starting out with a large number of contestants who share their sob stories with the viewers. The public would vote out contestants who display any hint of privilege or happiness. Poverty would be mandatory, as well as an alcoholic father, and most finalists will have been born into a family with more than ten children. The final would involve the remaining three contestants battling it out with stories of job losses and mortgage arrears. The series winner would clinch the prize when it emerges that their family home has dry rot, rising damp and subsidence levels so severe that they recently had to change their parish priest. In keeping with the show's theme, Barry's Tea would be the ideal sponsor for such a show. 'Barry's, putting the T into Torment'.

These reality shows would serve to unite the Irish family unit in these secular times. All family members would be glued to the screen, irrespective of age. (It should be noted that this obsession with hardship transcends generational barriers.) These shows would even have the power to overcome the current addiction to smartphones and social media. For one hour every week, Ireland's youth would be transfixed by the misery of others, so much so, in fact, that they would forget to tweet, text and snapchat images of their body parts. Previously estranged family members would weep and hug, forgiving any erstwhile slights and misdeeds. Empathy addiction is rife in this country, and there is nothing more uplifting for an Irish woman than feeling herself to be at one with the misfortunes of others.

⋎ The Big C ⋏

There are a number of C-words of relevance in Ireland. The C-word that is referred to as 'the big C', and not to be mistaken for 'the C-word' is, of course, Cancer. The entire female population of Ireland is pathologically obsessed with Cancer. There is no other disease that triggers their irrational fears quite like it. In fact, their superstitions are so pronounced that they will not even articulate the word 'Cancer'. Instead, the word is spoken in hushed, reverential tones. This behaviour stems from the well-known scientific fact that saying the word loudly actually triggers defective cell multiplication. Anyone who ever dies from Cancer was always discovered to be 'riddled' with it. This is an unusual turn of phrase, given that the disease itself does not cause bodily perforations. Be that as it may, an Irish woman will whisper the name of the condition but herald the announcement of the riddling it caused. The word is often repeated for maximum effect, as in:

'When they opened him up he was riddled, positively riddled with it.'

⚡ The Funeral Coat ⚡

When an Irish woman first hears that someone she knows has died, she will feel a momentary sadness and possibly even shed a tear. This is immediately replaced with panic. The Irish funeral is an important social event at which she must excel. There are protocols to be observed and rules that must be adhered to. No matter how grief-stricken the family of the deceased, they will notice flawed etiquette.

The first question that an Irish woman needs to ask is: 'Which outfit will I wear?' This is closely followed by: 'What state is my funeral coat in?' When Irish women get to a certain age, the purchase of a funeral coat is mandatory. Unlike a wedding outfit, you do not need to buy a new funeral coat for every funeral you attend, and spray tan is positively frowned upon.

Once an outfit has been chosen and the funeral coat located, you need to decide whether to attend the Removal or the Funeral Mass. The Removal is usually the quicker of the two. As it occurs in the evening, many opt for this event. However, if the deceased was a member of the GAA or a local politician, you could be queuing for hours at their Removal, by which time it will inevitably be raining. Take a moment to consider the popularity of the deceased and base your decision on that. Don't let the weather affect your decision – it will always be raining at an Irish funeral.

Removals usually take place at a funeral home, which is, invariably, a concrete bunker with dim lighting and no heat. The sub-zero temperature helps to preserve the body of the deceased. The dead person is placed in the middle of the room and their nearest and dearest stand in a semi-circle at one end. The director of the funeral home places crowd-control barriers in strategic positions, thereby corralling the mourners. This ensures that no one goes rogue and starts wandering off in the wrong direction.

Upon entering the room, mourners are presented with a comments book in which you're encouraged to write a brief platitude. This is not to be confused with the visitor's book in a hotel: 'Loving what you've done with the corpse' should be avoided at all costs.

The next concern will be what to say when you empathise with the relatives of the deceased. You could opt for the old reliable 'Sorry for your troubles,' but it is just so passé. You should really aim to say something deep and meaningful – memorable, even. After all, what is the point in taking time off work to get your hair straightened and your funeral coat dry-cleaned if no one is going to remember you? This is a tricky one. Unless you are a serial funeral attender, you will not be practised in the art of sincerity.

Other options include telling a short story about the last time you met the deceased. (Feel free to make something up; no one can contradict you.) There is no use in recounting a banal everyday experience like meeting up for coffee and a scone. Your final meeting with the deceased should have been a deep, philosophical moment with a life-enhancing message. This can drag on a bit though, especially if there is a queue of 400 mourners behind you. If you can't think of anything suitable yet snappy, log on to Facebook in advance and pick from the myriad funeral-friendly memes that people have posted there.

Most women cannot resist the urge to proclaim that they had predicted the imminent death. This can range from 'I was thinking he was looking a bit peaky' to 'I knew he wasn't long for this world'. Alternatively, you can shake your head and inanely state 'I don't know what to say,' to which the relative will reply 'There's nothing to say'. An awkward silence will ensue while they wait for you and your lack of imagination to move the fuck on.

⋏ Double-handed Handshake ⋏

It is a common occurrence that inexperienced funeral attendees find themselves lost for words at a funeral. They compensate by over-relying on the healing properties of human contact, which leads to the important question of just how much bodily contact is appropriate at a funeral? The level of physical contact has a direct correlation with how well you know the family of the deceased. This can sometimes be a little difficult to gauge, so here are some pointers:

* If you don't know the family member standing in front of you, then a single-handed handshake befits the situation.

* If you have met them once or twice, you could go for the double-handed handshake. Your two hands create a comforting enclosure that is meant to give solace to the bereaved. Additionally, you can give their entrapped hand a bit of a rattle when you want to emphasise a point.

* If you know the mourner well, you can up the physical contact. Superficial hugs are recommended. This is more of a cursory glancing of bodies, and can be accompanied with sympathetic mutterings. It is best to keep your mumblings at an inaudible level and pepper them with the word 'Sorry'. You will be in and out in seconds flat. By the time the bereaved realises that you have not actually formed a sentence you will have moved on to the next family member. Think of it as Speed Mourning.

* Let us imagine that the family member is a close personal friend. Full-contact hugs are now

permissable. However, you, the hugger, should never make the mistake of raising your arms above the hugee's shoulders. There is a thin line between an affectionate hug and a full-blown sexual assault. Nipple-to-nipple contact is never appropriate at a funeral, and there is no exception to this rule. If the bereaved is looking somewhat uncomfortable, or backing away slightly, you are probably overdoing it.

* Most Catholic Removals will have an open casket so that the mourners can pay their last respects. Try to avoid looking at the dead person if you can help it. It is physically possible to glance in the direction of the coffin with a quick movement of your head without actually focusing. This shouldn't be a problem as you will have perfected this movement during your driving test when you were pretending to check your mirrors. Try not to let your natural Irish female curiosity (euphemism alert) get the better of you. If you absolutely cannot resist, remember that the deceased will never look like the person you knew, unless you are attending the funeral of a drag queen. It does not matter if the deceased is an eighty-year-old farmer with hands like shovels, he will look like Priscilla, Queen of the Desert.

⚡ Griefometer ⚡

The funeral Mass is a slightly less intimidating affair. As the Irish population has been subjected to the ritual of Mass from a very young age, this episode is well within our comfort zone. Unless the priest is actually talking on a personal level about the deceased, it is customary to spend the hour glancing around the church to see who is there and what they are wearing. Some Irish women will even go to the trouble of using a griefometer to measure the level of mourning among the other attendees. The results can then be used to initiate small talk outside the church when the Mass is over.

Once outside, you will need to propel yourself towards any family members that you know in order to empathise with them. This is not as easy as it sounds as there will be at least 100 other people attempting to do the same thing. She who hesitates is lost; do not delay, and be as pushy as is necessary. Save the real aggression for the part-timers who sneaked in two minutes before the end of the Mass.

At this stage of the proceedings you will start to hear murmurs like 'Are ya going to the graveyard?', 'Can I've a lift?' with the odd 'Any fags?' thrown in for good measure. In the past, mourners would walk to the graveyard behind the hearse, but due to present levels of obesity and inclement weather, people usually drive. After parking at right angles to the pavement, you will now have to walk two miles uphill and stand in 100 mph crosswinds while the deceased is interred in their final resting place. This is a solemn affair, and many will take a moment to reflect on the circle of life. This pensive moment does not last long, however, as very quickly the murmur starts up again. This time it can be roughly translated as 'Are ya going to the hotel?', 'Can I've a lift?' with the occasional 'It's fuckin' Baltic' thrown in for good measure.

The minute you turn to leave the graveyard, the mood shifts dramatically. All thoughts of mortality are replaced with an overwhelming sense of relief. The sad funeral bit is over. There is no longer any pressure on an Irish woman to observe rituals and protocol. All that is required is that the deceased be given a proper send-off, which, as we all know, is code for heading straight to the hotel bar and getting shit-faced. This is a more free-form event at which an Irish woman excels.

Traditional Irish wakes involved a five-day piss-up during which many mourners would be arrested and many livers irreparably damaged. Sadly, this archaic form of send-off is no longer practised. We live in abstemious times, and these days the average funeral drinking session will only last for twelve hours. Now, a twelve-hour drinking session is not in itself unusual for an Irish woman, but the heady combination of relief and fatalism may have alarming consequences.

Firstly, her relationship with the deceased will grow in proportion to the number of drinks she has imbibed. By the time she is on her fifth G & T, the deceased will have been elevated from casual acquaintance to soulmate – so close was the bond between them that she will never get over their death. This delusion may prompt uncharacteristic honesty, and she may even feel compelled to tell her fellow mourners what she really thinks of them. Worse again, she may feel compelled to tell her fellow mourners what the deceased thought of them.

It has been an emotional day for everyone, so what better way to end it than to stand up and announce to the assembled mourners: 'He thought you were all a shower of bastards' Luckily, she will remember very little of the night's events. Upon waking the following morning, her primary concern will be what state her funeral coat is in.

⚡ Terminator Housekeeper ⚡

It is mostly Irish men who fall ill; Irish women simply do not have the time. Man Flu is a common predicament, but there is no similar ailment for the fairer sex.

It is a matter of pride with an Irish woman: she must never take to the bed with an ailment. An Irish woman could have pneumatic fever and multiple stab wounds and she would still be flat out performing her domestic chores. She is like the Terminator of Housekeepers and cannot be felled. 'Oh, don't mind me, it's just a flesh wound,' she will say, putting a fresh batch of scones into the oven while simultaneously bleeding all over the kitchen floor. It is a curious mixture of martyrdom and pride. Irish women are both fearful and scornful of sickness. This attitude is symptomatic of a time when survival of the fittest was a reality in this country.

The only affliction that an Irish woman will ever admit to is being stressed. Never just slightly stressed, always to the hilt. Of course, back in the 60s stress hadn't been invented so everyone had to make do with just being worried sick. If we skip back another generation, our grandmothers used to suffer dreadfully from their nerves. However, the one personality trait that transcends all generations is a savage dose of martyrdom.

⚡ The Seasonal C-word ⚡

The second pertinent C-word in Ireland is one that instantly elevates an Irish woman's toxic-stress levels.

This C-word can only be uttered for approximately eight weeks of every year, and is of course the heinous word 'Christmas'. If you dare utter this word any time during the ten-month period from 1 February to 30 November and within hearing range of an Irish female, she will turn on you with an unimaginable viciousness. Even whispering the word or making vague references to bearded men in red suits will bring on a tongue lashing that is directly at odds with an Irish woman's usual charming demeanour. The reason for this abhorrence is that once the word is uttered it's like an adrenaline shot to an Irish woman's heart. She is instantly propelled into a flurry of manic consumerist activity.

Firstly, she will need to hire a small articulated lorry and park it right outside the front door of the nearest toy store. Once inside, she will spend an average of €800 on shiny, breakable, plastic shite and forget to buy the obligatory sackload of batteries so that Christmas morning is a total disaster with her husband calling her a moron and her children crying hysterically because Santa hates them and is punishing them by giving them toys that do not work.

Her next task is to park the obscene vehicle as close as possible to the nearest Marks & Spencer's. Although she is just nipping in to stock up on nibbles in case any of the neighbours drop by over the festive season, she will likely fall prey to the 3-for-2 consumer-confidence scam. This will result in her spending a further €300 on cocktail sausages and miniature Peking duck. By the time she has finished shopping, spring-cleaning her house and cooking solidly for a thirty-six-hour period, she will be suffering from physical and mental exhaustion, and it's still only 12 August.

⚡ Queen of Busyness ⚡

Most Irish women are under the impression that no one suffers as they do and that no one on the planet works as hard as them. They are extremely competitive about their busyness, and become vicious if anyone suggests that they have been relaxing or having any leisure time. This lends itself to some very snarky conversations. When two Irish women bump into each other on the street, they must stake their busyness claims before moving on to less confrontational topics.

Both will allege that they are 'up the feckin' walls' and that they 'haven't stopped going all week'. Each woman will then give an account of how many hours of overtime they've worked, what household chores they've done, their pick-ups and drop-offs, how many mouths they've fed and how many sick children, parents or neighbours they've had to nurse back to health. Florence Nightingale would baulk at such a schedule.

Then, one woman might raise the stakes by throwing in a midweek visit to the Accident and Emergency. Given that you lose approximately twenty-eight hours of your life during a visit to the A & E, it's a hard one to best in the horrifically busy stakes – A & E woman is clearly edging out in front. Her opponent parries with the news that a group of distant relatives from the USA are staying in her house for the week, making her the undisputed champion. Everyone knows that the high-maintenance visiting Yanks will consume an untold number of days with excursions to Connemara, the Cliffs of Moher, the never-ending trips around the Ring of Kerry, the unsuccessful search for the elusive XXL-sized Aran jumper, frying sausages and black pudding every morning and the obligatory drinking of pints and listening to trad music every night. Visiting Yanks woman steals the day. She is the crowned Queen of Busyness, leaving A & E woman to admit defeat, albeit ungraciously.

*

The good news is that Irish women are starting to take small steps towards the practice of self-care. These women gorged themselves on negativity during the recession, and the post-recessionary hangover has caused them to lose their appetite for misery. They are becoming less comfortable with the misfortune of others. Also, Irish women are no longer convinced that looking after their own emotional and physical health is selfish, slothful and overly indulgent. They are gradually throwing off the martyrdom mantle, and may even be able to say no to someone, somewhere in the not too distant future, although they'll never say no to making the sandwiches for a funeral.

3.
The Bold and the Beautiful

In the mid nineteenth century, an English anthropological journal claimed that Gaelic people were characterised by bulging jaws, a retreating chin, a large mouth, thick lips, sunken eyes and protruding ears. The perception of Irish people as simian imbeciles was typical of colonial stereotyping. We were like an island of extreme makeover contestants, eagerly awaiting the arrival of shows like *The Swan*. In our defence, we had good reason to be ugly: Irish peasants suffered from chronic malnutrition and existed in abject poverty, not to mention the severe narrowing of our gene pool brought about by mass emigration and a million deaths from famine.

While there was the occasional genetic windfall, like the arrival of the Spanish Armada in 1588, alas, a handful of Spanish sailors were no match for the libidinous local lads. All the sallow skin and swarthy good looks had been bred out of Ireland within a couple of generations. Periodically, a child is still born in the Claddagh with a monobrow and a pronounced lisp, but otherwise all traces of our Spanish visitors have been eradicated.

⋏ Warty Nora ⋌

In the good old days, a plague of ugly people skulked through the streets of Ireland, humpbacked, cross-eyed, peg-legged and moley-faced – such mutations were considered quite normal. In Ireland we celebrate mingers and treat our winos like rock stars. Most Irish towns still have a number of resident 'characters'. The female ones are always called Nora, Bridget or Annie, and are usually given pet names such as 'Scary Annie' or 'Warty Nora'. These women are the physical embodiment of Disney's wicked witch, complete with headscarf, pointy chin, hooked noses and an array of hairy moles. Their four remaining teeth clamp vice-like around a soggy cigarette butt as they let forth a torrent of expletives. Women who look like Nora or Annie often approach small children, pat them on the head, and inform the terrified youngster that they must come home with them and live with them forever. This is perfectly acceptable behaviour in Ireland, and phoning the authorities is considered a gross overreaction.

These women are national treasures, and rightly so. People lavish them with gifts of fresh cigarettes or the price of a pint. If one such woman spits on you, it is considered to be extremely lucky. Sadly, such characters are in danger of extinction. An increase in disposable income and the rise of the Irish beauty industry are threatening the very existence of Warty Nora and her ilk. They're an endangered species, but, with the help of a Mind the Minger campaign, they may stand some chance of survival. Such campaigns might involve:

* A well-executed photo shoot showing them in their natural environment to raise awareness of their plight.

* A commemorative Warty Nora edition postage stamp to help raise vital funds.

* A day-in-the-life RTÉ production. The ladies would be paid in scratch cards (to which they are extremely partial). Benson & Hedges would be ideally placed as sponsors. The camera crew could

film them reading the fortunes of unsuspecting tourists and extorting money for 7Up bottles of 'holy' water – only a tenner a go.

Ireland is at risk of becoming Nora-less and turning into a generic European country. We need our Noras to remind us of who we are, and, more importantly, of what went before....

In 2003, Rosanna Davison was crowned Miss World and claimed Ireland's first beauty pageant title. Irrespective of how you feel about beauty pageants, this was a momentous feat. We had come a long way: from the iconic Peig Sayers, with her weather-beaten face and threadbare shawl, to the swimsuit-clad Barbie-doll beauty of Miss World. Now, you could argue that Rosanna is not your typical Irish woman and should have been disqualified, being the blonde-haired, brown-eyed daughter of an Argentinian hobbit. Nonetheless, for the first time in history, an Irish woman was adjudged more beautiful than any other nationality.

⋀ Oxymoron ⋀

However, the term 'Irish beauty' is still considered to be an oxymoron. Occasionally, gorgeous Irish girls are born, but, by and large, Irish women suffer from Short Stature, Freckly Skin and Crooked Teeth.

* **Short Stature:** Stately Amazonian types are few and far between in this country, and Short Stature has actually been proven to be an evolutionary trait. Thanks to centuries spent crouched over picking rancid potatoes and bowing to Catholic priests, most Irish women are short-arsed. With increased secularisation and current nutritional awareness, we are now producing much taller offspring. The key to this is less grovelling and more protein shakes.

* **Freckly Skin:** All the women who feature in Celtic mythology are described as having milky white complexions. Foreigners often think that Irish women have beautiful pale skin, and while it could be argued that we do have skin of alabaster, unfortunately it is hidden under a mass of freckles. From a very young age, Irish girls are intent on removing this physical imperfection. At the mere hint of warm weather, we strip off, spread Frytex all over our bodies and wrap ourselves in tinfoil. We'd even impale ourselves on a remote-controlled spit if we thought it would assist the tanning process. It's a desperate bid to join the dots. This reckless version of sunbathing leads to second-degree

burns and excessive peeling, which results in even more freckles, not to mention the occasional life-threatening mole. Today, Ireland has one of the highest skin cancer rates in the world. Melanoma is a reality and not a Spice Girl.

* **Thin Brown Hair:** There is a further misconception that Irish women have long, thick red hair. In reality, most Irish girls are born with wispy, mousy brown hair. Also, as a result of our damp climate, Irish women suffer from horrifically frizzy locks. All we have to do is glance in the direction of cumulus clouds and our hair rises and expands of its own volition. Static electricity is our enemy; large bodies of water and trampolines should be avoided at all costs. This is not easy when you live on a windswept island in the North Atlantic, where, during the decadent Noughties, a trampoline, a Belfast sink and a wrap-around deck were considered mandatory adornments to the average abode.

As we are now painfully aware, what goes up must come down. Of course, being Irish, there is always a more feral edge to our middle-class ways. We tend to take a relaxed approach to such trampoline safety recommendations as removing your shoes and limiting use to no more than two children at a time. In our fair land, troops of children can be seen arming themselves with hurls and bats before climbing onto the trampoline. Parents, in the meantime, are busy sedating themselves with a cheeky Bordeaux in an attempt to quell their money worries. Mummy is lounging on the deck with her frizzy hair, flushed cheeks and telltale red wine stains on her teeth. She barely even notices the M.M.A. cage fighting that is being carried out by her offspring.

Crooked Teeth: Cosmetic dental practice is relatively new in Ireland. Prior to the 1990s, Irish children born with prominent or crooked teeth were resigned to their fate, and the teenage years spent swigging back MiWadi and chain-smoking Majors only compounded this dental disaster. Like twenty-four-hour shopping and gun fatalities, straight white teeth had not yet made their way across the Atlantic – we only ever caught sight of them on weekly episodes of *Dallas* or *Falcon Crest*. They could also be glimpsed when American relatives were visiting with their dazzling white smiles and tartan polyester pants. In the ensuing family photos, all the Irish kids look like scowling peasants. They were, in fact, hiding their teeth. You can relate to this if you've ever had your photo taken beside an American. The dental comparison is not kind.

⚡ Home Beauty Practices ⚡

But Irish women are nothing if not resilient. Cursed by these physical misfortunes, we set about reversing them. The emergence of the beauty industry as a multi-million euro business in Ireland is a recent phenomenon. Growing up in the 80s, there were very few options available to young Irish girls who wished to correct their fugly features, and attempts at home remedies were an unmitigated disaster.

One recommended cure for frizzy hair was to lay your head down on the ironing board and literally iron your locks straight. What could be simpler? In fact, this was quite a risky practice. Occasionally the home beauty practitioner would move the iron too close to their head and burn their ear off. A more frequent occurrence was leaving the iron on your hair for too long and singeing your tresses so that you ended up looking like one of those grotesque Troll dolls with a rigid, synthetic mane.

During their teens, Irish girls tend to go through a phase of eyebrow fixation. In hindsight, badly shaped eyebrows were the least of our problems. Nonetheless, we would spend countless painful afternoons attempting to sculpt the perfect brow. There were always at least three teenage girls present: the client (read: guinea pig), the self-designated depilatory expert and a surgical assistant who doubled as brow critic. The standard brow-shaping tools were a rusty tweezers or some Nair hair-removal cream. The brow team would be oblivious to the fact that Nair was primarily intended to remove hair from the bikini zone and would anxiously spread the odorous ooze around the periphery of the offending eyebrows.

The Nair cream was always stolen from the mirrored press above the sink in a parent's bathroom, the sacred place reserved for the pills and creams that represented the mysteries of adult life. There was always the danger that the depilatory expert would misread the label and that, ten minutes later, the client's entire face would be covered in rapidly growing pubic hair. Luckily, the Nair was completely ineffectual and just left you with a forehead that smelt like a vagina instead of a face that looked like one.

Today's young Irish girls wouldn't be seen dead without a strong eyebrow game. They recognise the monumental importance of a good brow shape for the face. This was not always the case among the pre-iPhone generations, when eyebrow maintenance was considered to be relatively inconsequential, maybe on a par with having your toenails painted, but definitely nowhere near as life or death as having a symmetrical Farrah Fawcett flick. But the brow has evolved from mono to HD. It is remarkable how the powers of the HD brow can transform the face of the home brow practitioner from the over-plucked, permanently alarmed and slightly psychotic look, to the vision of Hollywood celebrity perfection – merely by the removal of a couple of stray hairs combined with some pretty basic colouring in. The female population of Ireland are anxiously awaiting the emergence of 3D brows.

The bleaching of non-existent moustaches was another firm favourite. All hail Jolene, a product that smelt like the school toilets but came with a spatula and a mixing tray, thus adding a much-needed air of professionalism to home beauty proceedings. The first step involved a small amount of Jolene being applied over the upper lip. During the recommended ten-minute interval there was a slight tingling sensation, but any results were invisible to the naked eye. A second application was attempted. This time, a liberal amount of cream was applied and an hour was agreed to be a suitable waiting period. The tingling sensation returned, closely followed by an intense burning sensation. In true martyrdom fashion, scalding was endured. After one hour, the cream was washed off and the tache was found to be several shades lighter. Unfortunately, the surrounding skin had also been bleached and the overall effect was verging on piebald.

The Debs

During the pre-beauty parlour era, all DIY practices were considered to be the dress rehearsal for the one major beauty event in a young Irish girl's life: The Debs. This was an occasion where beauty preparation had a manic intensity. Most girls purchased their *gúna deas* well in advance and had an arsenal of beauty solutions at the ready.

The standard titillating toolbox of the day contained a shaping kit for eyebrows and some tanning tablets that were 'guaranteed' to give you a golden glow. The tablets were to be taken around lunchtime on the day of the event so that they'd kick in on time. The next step involved careful ironing of the hair so that there was no visible scarring. Then all that remained was to fashion the shapely brows. The revolutionary brow kit contained a number of mini wax strips that were supposed to remove the stray hairs and leave the glamorous eyebrow behind.

There were always a couple of girls who were overzealous with their wax strips and ended up whipping off an entire eyebrow. Horrific as this sounds, there was usually someone worse off in the beauty stakes. We all know the one poor unfortunate who overplayed their tanning game. Half an hour before kick off, the pill-popper would suddenly notice that all was not well on the tanning front. There was a distinctly orange hue to the palms of her hands. This awareness would cause her to break out in a cold sweat shortly followed by an involuntary rectal contraction as she realised the colour was spreading. This glow was more tandoori than golden, and it would inevitably get stronger. On the most important night of a young Irish gal's life, as the synthesised strains of 'Hungry Like the Wolf' filled the dance hall, the scene lent itself more to *Willy Wonka* than *Cinderella*.

The arrival of fake tan in the late 80s brought the Dawn of a New Age. Historians consider the Renaissance to be the beginning of the modern era. Similarly, the emergence of Johnson's Holiday Skin heralded the arrival of the modern Irish woman. Like all rebirths, there were a certain number of teething problems to contend with. Initial application skills were limited. You could tell a girl's level of experience by the shade of her knees and elbows. After a bit of practice, the Irish woman mastered the art of avoidance: joints and the neck area were left well alone. Even now, only the most experienced users will risk home tanning their feet. As any decent plasterer will tell you, preparation is key. Time spent on exfoliation and moisturising pays off. This can be the difference between looking sun-kissed and fabulous in your little black number as opposed to the mottled Tangoed look endemic to modern Irish weddings.

⋏ Da Bootay ⋌

Up until recently, the Irish arse had led a relatively sheltered existence, having spent the 40s and 50s hidden beneath a shapeless floral housecoat. There was a brief spell of incarceration within the woollen twinset that proved a bit itchy and sweaty and necessitated some furtive scratching, although always in the privacy of an Irish woman's home. During the 60s, it was widely felt that as long as the Irish arse was accessorised with a nice pair of shoes and a matching handbag, then all was well in the world. The revolutionary leap to slacks and jeans during the 70s and 80s gave the Irish arse a new identity as the bondage-free buttocks took on a definitive size and shape. This was a period when the well-endowed arse would usually be covered up with a long top. The smaller, more petite version would be shown off to its full advantage being pummelled into some skintight stonewashed denims. During the 90s, the focus moved up to the belly, as crop tops and low-rise jeans were the order of the day. The Irish arse was virtually forgotten until the recent cataclysmic emergence of da Bootay. The Irish backside is now back with a vengeance. Skinny heroin-chic no-arses are SO last season; the big, bountiful butt is best. Having spent decades trying to cover itself up or shed those resistant pounds, the Irish arse is now protruding proudly in all its glory. Latin and African American cultures have always preferred a bigger booty, and hip-hop and R & B stars have been extolling the virtues of a grand-sized arse for more than twenty years, but all that has moved into Irish popular culture now. The sale of Penney's butt pads is living proof of how mainstream da Bootay has become. If an Irish woman does not naturally have the requisite curves, she can purchase herself some shape-wear in the form of butt pad underwear, sucky-inneys and waist-training corsets. Failing that, partially inflating a couple of beach balls and subsequently ratchet strapping them into place should secure your voluptuous cargo.

Now that a decent derrière has come into prominence, it seems only natural that it would flaunt its new-found status in the form of twerking. For the uninitiated, twerking refers to a type of dancing in which an individual, usually a female, dances to music in a sexually provocative manner involving thrusting hip movements, rapid successive shaking of da Bootay and a low squatting stance. Irish women are not prone to overtly sexual behaviour and, sadly, the practice of twerking does not come as naturally to them as their Latin American counterparts. In order to even attempt a twerk, an Irish girl would have to be blind-drunk, epileptic and home alone. Dancing in a circle with their friends with the occasional hilarious foray into the YMCA dance routine or the more complex Macarena moves is sufficiently sexy for your average Irish gal.

There is a tendency among people of a certain age to regard their youthful looks with nostalgia. Baz Luhrmann advised 'in twenty years, you'll look back at photos of yourself and recall in a way you can't grasp now how much possibility lay before you and how fabulous you really looked'. Baz has obviously never seen this author's Confirmation snaps. These days, it doesn't actually matter if you're born with crooked teeth, sticky out ears and a tache worthy of Magnum PI – it can all be sorted! You can be plucked, waxed, bleached and ionised. You can enter the beauty salon looking like Warty Nora, pay a hefty sum and emerge a Rosanna Davison.

We have become a nation of flawless, straight-haired pouters. For the first time ever, we are verging on symmetry. Irish women are no longer ugly! The selfie epidemic can be seen as a celebration of our newly acquired beauty. It's all boutique hotels, Botox, designer clothes and furless fannies, or was that furless clothes and designer fannies? Vagazzling – the bejewelling of the punani – is relatively new to these shores. And if you're wondering whether you should get on board this trend, ask yourself: how would Peig Sayers react to vagazzling?:

* Lift the taypot from the hearth;

* Goile in the chickens;

* Close the gate behind her and trek ten miles to the top of the nearest mountain; then

* Strap her twenty-two children to her back and hurl herself off that mountain.

4.
The Ballroom of Romance

The Romantic Journey of the Hibernian Harlot

There is no doubt that sex and sexuality have drastically changed over the last few generations. Ireland has undergone the Revolution of the Ride, resulting in sex becoming mainstream and pornography being available on tap. Today's news headlines read like 1970s porn movie titles: 'Sexting in the Seanad', 'Human Sex Trafficking in the Midlands', 'Debbie does Dingle'. On the plus side, thanks to fibre-optic broadband – bestiality seems to be virtually obsolete.

In 1913, William Butler Yeats stated that 'Romantic Ireland's dead and gone'. Is it possible that he was predicting a time when the walk of shame was commonplace?

Or perhaps he was referring to the alleged practice of 'hedging' where young Irish girls lurk in the bushes to remove their knickers before entering the school disco. (Ironically, during the seventeenth century, these hedges were full of besieged Catholic children hiding out from their oppressors in an attempt to procure an education.)

⚡ The Summer of Love ⚡

While these extremes highlight the monumental changes in Ireland, it is also surprising to think that arranged marriages were common practice and lawyers were still drawing up marriage contracts in the 1980s. Similarly, not many people know that the Famine changed the way in which marriage and courting were practised in Ireland. In pre-Famine days, people in Ireland married for love without any concern for The Land. While the rest of Europe was busy with the Napoleonic Wars, the Irish were flat out too. In 1800, the population in Ireland was approximately five million. By 1841, it had risen to over eight million. The pre-Famine generation married in their twenties or younger without a thought for their future source of income. There was plenty of spare land, and they could head off and literally 'bag' themselves a few acres and settle down to marital bliss. It was the Irish equivalent of the Summer of Love, complete with untold amounts of poitín and the sacrilegious practice of free love. Naturally, all this happiness and alcohol resulted in a doubling of the population and a reduction in the size of the land holdings. If you drive through Connemara today, you can see all the postage-stamp-sized fields surrounded by rickety stone walls. These are a direct result of the shagfest pre 1845.

⋔ Love and the Land ⋏

Alas, it wasn't to last. The dreaded blight descended and, as a result, both during and after the Famine, marriage became a commercial, rather than a biological, affair. A classic slag today when Irish girls are telling their buddies about a recent conquest is 'Does he own any land?' or 'Any road frontage?' but it wasn't too long ago that these were serious considerations. You had a Bull McCabe at the head of every Irish family whose only concern was The Land. Romantic love was pretty low down on their list of priorities. Getting the land – and keeping it within the family – was all that mattered, irrespective of the consequences. This resulted in the dubious Irish practice of marrying your first cousin. Sure, if the Pope gave it his blessing then it must be all right. As if mass emigration and countless deaths from starvation weren't bad enough, you had widespread interbreeding to contend with.

Emma Comerford

So, the father owned The Land and therefore held all the power. He very rarely passed it on to his eldest son until he was on death's door. He also exploited this power by choosing whom his son should marry. The choice of a suitable wife from a father's perspective was based on some pretty definite criteria:

* She should be strong and submissive – strong enough to carry a sickly calf on her back but submissive enough not to bludgeon her in-laws to death; and

* She should be fertile and well skilled in domestic duties – the usual duties that require multi-tasking such as baking bread and mopping floors while simultaneously giving birth to healthy male grandchildren.

These minimum requirements could, in fact, be overlooked if the girl in question came with a field. She could be a syphilitic, non-Y-chromosome-producing degenerate whore with Paris Hilton's housekeeping skills and Naomi Campbell's personality so long as she brought a few acres to the table.

A man who married someone based on her wealth or property was said to have 'married in'. Previous generations would often utter the likes of: 'Your uncle Seamus *married in* to that farm'. There would be a brief

62

pause then someone would elaborate that 'his new wife, Betty, has a birthmark on her face in the shape of the Persian Empire', the implication being that Seamus would never have married her if it wasn't for the land.

⋋ Matchmakers ⋌

It was during this era of arranged marriages that the role of the matchmaker became prominent in Irish society. The self-appointed matchmaker could be male or female, and was very often a publican. Every Irish village had a practising matchmaker; presumably the female matchmakers looked like the legendary Cilla Black but were dressed like Queen Victoria with a lace doily on their heads.

The modern-day role of matchmaker has been taken over by the likes of Paddy McGuinness or Ireland's own Ray Foley, and the *Take Me Out* TV franchise is quite formulaic. It can be summed up as follows:

* Every week a tall and patronising host introduces a series of single men for public humiliation.

* The bevy of beauties consists of nine mingers, two slappers and the obligatory classy burd.

* The evening's entertainment begins with some cringeworthy double entendres.

* The men are then subjected to the type of cold, calculating scrutiny normally reserved for livestock at the Ballinasloe Horse Fair.

* Cue more hilarious double entendres.

* Usually the guys start off quite well. They are easy on the eye and assume the classic 'cheeky chappie' persona. However, it isn't long before we discover that they live at home with their mammy, have four children from four previous relationships and are currently unemployed but hoping to make some money breeding pit bulls.

* All the women turn off their lights except the two slappers. No matter how cute and happy-go-lucky the guy appeared previously, he will now look like a pathetic loser.

* He picks the better looking of the two girls. If there isn't much between them, then he will opt for the one showing the most cleavage.

* The happy couple skip off into the sunset, and there is just enough time for one more round of hilarious double entendres before they roll out the next victim.

⚡ Ballroom of Romance ⚡

During the 1950s and 60s in Ireland, young people found love at dances in ballrooms and parochial halls. When we hear stories about romance during the showband era, it's as alien to us as the mating rituals practised by native tribes in Papua New Guinea. It is hard to imagine the attraction as there was no alcohol and you had to cycle at least ten miles to even get there. Yet people flocked to hundreds of ballrooms located in the cities and spread out across the country. Sometimes the hall in question was literally in the middle of nowhere, or at a point where two country roads crossed. Perhaps, unbeknownst to the majority of the Irish population, there are a series of invisible songlines across the Irish landscape, which possibly guided the acid house practitioners in their choice of rave locations some forty years later.

But the Irish girls of the showband era were a far cry from neon mesh vests and glow stick accessories. They dressed in felt skirts with layers of petticoats worn underneath. The petticoats were sprinkled with sugar to stiffen them and get the desired lift when the jive, waltz or foxtrot would kick in.

Jiving was probably the most important of the dances, and is part of Ireland's rural genetic memory, along with an inexplicable love of Garth Brooks. On the night of the dance, there would usually be a resident band and a headline act. The resident band would play the songs in sets of three to provide the opportunity for dance partners to get better acquainted. The women would line up against the wall on one side of the ballroom and the men would take up position along the opposite wall. The dance floor in the middle was a sexual no man's land.

Once the band struck up, the men would move forward in a line to advance, commencing the battle of the sexes. Although the dance halls didn't serve alcohol, the men would be well tanked up beforehand, which helped stiffen them and get the desired lift. Being paralytic from drink also eased the humiliation of rejection should they be refused a dance. As the halls were packed full of a heaving mass of bodies with little or no ventilation, the 'Ask me sister, I'm sweatin' rejection tactic was born. The fact that a potential dance partner was shit-faced would be overlooked if he was cute or known to be an excellent jiver, which proves that Irish women were just as shallow and misguided back then as they are now.

If all was going well between the newly acquainted dance partners, the Irish girl would be asked if she wanted to go for a mineral. This was the old-fashioned version of 'Grab your coat, love, you've pulled' or 'Should I call you or nudge you?' In William Trevor's *Ballroom of Romance*, much was made of the sexploits of the day, but the reality was that trying to negotiate any body part through layers of petticoats proved difficult. Similarly, all the twisting and jiving caused an excess of perspiration, which melted the sugar, causing a candyfloss effect. The end result was impenetrable; the local lads would have needed a mining helmet and a machete to make any headway. And so, the girls ended up stepping out with their chosen jive partner, limiting all sexual activity to frenzied snogging and the odd grope in a hallway until their wedding night.

⚡ Shifting ⚡

Along came the 80s and, with it, the semantic invention of shifting. A shift was a brilliant generalisation as it encompassed anything from a half-hearted snog to full-blown sex. Irish girls could inform a group of friends that they had shifted someone the night before and they would be none the wiser.

The shifting scene was often preceded with a number of years' internship, when Irish girls were first exposed to boys who were neither neighbours nor cousins.

Some kids sniff glue, others go hedging ... but 80s' kids went roller skating. Skates, legwarmers and shite music were the cultural resources of the day, and the combination of foot odour and stale carpet smells seemed to chemically combine to induce the onset of puberty. After approximately half an hour's skating to Boney M and Cliff Richard, all of a sudden the lights would dim and a slow set would begin. A bomb scare would have induced less panic. There was always a frenzied stampede as everyone rushed to exit the dance floor. It was mayhem, with the smaller teenagers getting trampled under skate. There was nothing in the world as humiliating as being the poor bastard who had just passed the exit and had to skate all the way back around the dance floor on their own in the middle of a slow set. This was a social degradation from which you might never recover. It brought back memories of playing musical chairs: a fun game played at young children's birthday parties that introduces them to social exclusion at an early age.

Most 80s' girls attended their local roller disco every Saturday afternoon, and being asked out for 'a slow dance' was a rite of passage. This consisted of holding your partner's hand and roller skating for the duration of the song without uttering a word to one another. Once the excitement of being asked to dance had dissipated, the girl was often vaguely disappointed with her dance partner's appearance. Nonetheless, she was confident that they were on the verge of a social triumph and visions of a roller disco themed wedding reception would begin to flash in her pubescent mind.

In reality, the roller skating skills of the couple were often badly mismatched. The Irish lad often had to half drag his dance partner along behind him. Being pulled along created an unwanted momentum and she would pick up speed. There would inevitably be a Torville and Dean moment when both youngsters skated alongside each other, but this vision of synchronicity was brief. The Irish girl would end up careening off ahead of her dance partner while still holding his hand. At the roller disco, many hearts were broken and multiple injuries sustained.

↘ Spin the Bottle ↗

It wasn't long before the roller disco had been replaced with a much more exciting hobby in the form of Spin the Bottle. Many Irish kids spent their teenage years learning important skills such as how to light a cigarette in torrential rain and gale-force winds and how to French kiss expertly. They would play a number of decadent games such as Spin the Bottle, Truth or

Dare, or Chicken. The games were usually played sitting on the damp grass in a field or in a dilapidated old caravan.

Spin the Bottle was a straightforward snogging game. The main problem was the shortage of eligible boys/prospective snogging partners in the vicinity. There were usually approximately eight teenagers sitting in a circle with a manky bottle placed carefully in the centre. It is quite difficult to find a nice flat field in Ireland, so there were always a few false starts with the bottle rolling off down a hill. The bottle was spun around and the boy closest to the top of the bottle had to kiss the girl closest to the bottom of the bottle or vice versa. There was no same-sex kissing, not because teens were opposed to that sort of thing but because it genuinely never dawned on them. After three rounds of kissing the same boy, you could try to fix the outcome, but it was difficult to do. A complex algorithm probably existed where the gravitational force multiplied by the bottle's circumference would give you the necessary trajectory for spinning the bottle, but no Irish teenager could ever work it out.

There was far more pressure on the boys during these games as they were expected to take the lead, and it wasn't long before certain types of kissing practices emerged:

* **The Plunger:** this type of kisser would suction themselves onto the lower half of your face and literally suck the face off you. Some young lads took this a step too far; girls' fillings were dislodged and internal organs misplaced. Plunging was very painful, and faces would emerge red and blotchy after one of these hooverings.

* **The Drooler:** there was always an excess of saliva when a drooler kissed you. They would thrust their tongue into your mouth and slobber, ad nauseum, with their thick, jellied lips. This type of snog was reminiscent of an Irish Mammy's attempt to forcefeed her children liver. You had to discreetly dry your face on your sleeve before the approach of your next suitor.

* **The Snake:** his technique was the polar opposite to the drooler. The kiss commenced with a long, drawn out, gnawing experience. There was no discernible salivary involvement. Just when you had lost the will to live, there would be a sudden darting movement of the tongue similar to a viper under threat. This unexpected tongue assault woke you up with a jolt. Then the gnawing would continue indefinitely and you would be lulled back into a false sense of security. All this

gnawing and darting was very unsettling and bad for the nerves.

⚡ Chicken ⚡

Chicken was a 'copping a feel' game. Again, the rules were straightforward. The boy in question would start by placing his hand on your knee and ask 'Are ya chicken?' When you assured them that you weren't, he would move his hand a bit further up your thigh and ask 'Now, are ya chicken?' The game continued in this manner until their hand had reached the top of your thigh – within reach of his intended destination. At this point, all your inbuilt Catholic alarm bells would start ringing. The outcome of this important moral decision was undoubtedly influenced by the fact that you were surrounded by at least five other teenagers and, in many cases, at least two would be blood relatives. The group would hold their breath in collective anticipation, then, when you replied in the affirmative, there would be a communal sigh of disappointment. It was rare to see a girl allow the boy's hand to travel into the demilitarised zone as the combined influence of Catholic dogma and witnesses proved a powerful preventative. Chicken was considered to be the most shocking and risqué of teenage endeavours in the 1980s.

⚡ Truth or Dare ⚡

Truth or Dare, which could have been a thrilling pastime, was in reality disappointing. Most young teens were hindered by their lack of imagination and the absence of any decent secrets in their lives. The truth question usually involved being asked if you fancied Fintan more than Dermott – it was hardly The Hague.

Usually the dares weren't overly taxing and involved having to snog Fintan or Dermott, or both Fintan and Dermott – but never at the same time. As previously mentioned, it just didn't dawn on Irish teenagers to liven up the kissing with any same-sex antics; in fact, Irish television didn't screen its first gay kiss until *Fair City* took the plunge in 1996. On the very rare occasion when kids had had enough of all the jawing, they would dare each other to ring a neighbour's doorbell or raid someone's orchard. These dares were way better craic than exchanging saliva with pimply youths, though few would ever admit to this. These were carefree, exciting times before one's conscience became burdened with empathy. You can lecture a teenager about mature conduct and neighbourly relations and they will gaze back at you with the apathetic stare of a seasoned psychopath. It's not that they don't realise how offensive/annoying/childish their behaviour is, it's just that they don't give a shit.

Sometimes, introducing a time frame enhanced the risk of the dare. For example, you might have to keep your finger on the doorbell for a certain length of time. The dare giver might pick the crankiest bastard in the village and dare you to ring their doorbell for a count of thirty and off you'd trot, digit at the ready. The Irish teen would be petrified standing in broad daylight with their finger stuck to the doorbell, partly deafened by the incessant pealing. They would just about hear the homeowner's approach over the noise, the adrenaline rush would kick in and they would bolt through the garden and hurdle over their wall with the speed and agility of an Olympian. It was totally exhilarating. Most Irish teenagers who indulged in this type of behaviour ended up with substance abuse problems in later life.

⋏ Serious Relationships ⋌

The years passed, and Irish girls started to have proper boyfriends. Initially they would be approached by a boy who lived in the same area and asked if they would 'go' with their friend. The girl may not even know her prospective boyfriend, but she always agreed. In the absence of any means of communication, she had to rely on sheer luck to meet up with her new swain. After a week she would have lengthy, agonising discussions with her friends about the romance, proclaiming that she just wasn't ready to be tied to a serious relationship. The girl would then approach some random young lad and ask them if they knew her boyfriend and, if they did, could they tell him that it was 'off'.

The whole affair could be conducted from start to finish without either party actually meeting their other half, which tended to ease the heartbreak of separation. Once the affairs of the heart became more tangible the break-ups were less trivial. Typical reasons for ending a romance included not liking the colour of his shoes/jumper/hair, being asked out by another unidentified young lad, not being into the same music and being physically repulsed by their kissing technique (see Spin the Bottle section).

Dating someone for a three-week period without ever casting eyes on them is antithetical to the modern-day practice of cyberstalking. Today's single Irish girl spends hours in front of a screen, fiendishly scouring the internet for snippets of information about a potential shift. By the time she casually bumps into him in his local pub (spotted in the background of his Instagram profile) she will already know more about him than his own mother, who presumably cannot recite his Facebook posts from memory and has never seen his penis on Snapchat.

⋎ Creeping ⋏

How do you differentiate between a healthy interest and full-blown stalking? If at any point you find that it's 2 a.m. and you are casually clicking through the photos of his sister's friend's cousin's newborn baby on Facebook, then you are creeping hard. Accidentally liking a holiday photo from his Magaluf 2010 trip is a social faux pas from which you will never recover. Should that happen at any point, it is probably a good time to reconsider that overseas volunteering place-ment. Poverty tourism is very popular at the moment, and becoming a volunteer for the construction of a schoolhouse in a Masai village in Tanzania is the only way to redeem yourself and distract everyone with your altruism and generosity of spirit. Once you arrive in the village, you may find that they have very basic levels of comfort and hygiene, no time for even the most rudimentary eyebrow maintenance, and internet coverage will likely be non-existent. Any visions you had of upping your Insta-game with photos of your-self sitting under a tree giving English classes to the adorable local kids will sadly fade as it immediately becomes apparent that you have no teaching qualifications and that your building skills are worthless. In fact, the only job you are capable of doing is putting the finishing coat of paint on the completed building. The Masai elders may even respectfully suggest that the NGO who organised the placement stop wasting everyone's time and just donate the price of the flights in the future.

⚡ Sex in the 80s and Beyond ⚡

The most shocking sex event in the late 80s was when the artist formely known as Prince writhed and gyrated all over a grand piano in Páirc Uí Chaoimh in Cork. He was like a pampered chihuahua in heat, and his Irish female fans couldn't get enough of him. Sex education in Ireland during this period could be paraphrased as 'Handy hints for dealing with sex-crazed schoolboys'. Accoutrements were key: teenage girls were advised never to leave home without a bicycle and a copy of the Golden Pages. If a boy walked you home, you were to ensure the bicycle was positioned between yourself and the lecherous youth. Similarly, if he tried to get you to sit on his lap, the trusty Golden Pages was to be placed between yourself and the offending region. In hindsight, getting sex advice from Irish nuns was like getting dental hygiene tips from Shane McGowan.

Most carnal knowledge transfers happened in the school playground. This is where Irish teenagers first heard about crabs. Not for them the vile threats of chlamydia, gonorrhoea and genital warts. The only STD in Ireland in the 80s was crabs. Although the name was slightly comical, the 80s' kids were surprisingly apprehensive.

The rumours abounded: you could catch them from toilet seats or from using an infected bath towel. Suddenly every teenage girl started to hover while pissing. They could be seen loitering in the vicinity of the hot press, covertly inspecting the laundry.

Everyone was a potential carrier, and innocent household items became a threat:

* What if a crab carrier had wiped themselves with the facecloth in the bathroom and you inadvertently cleaned your face with it?

* What if this half-crazed carrier went on a wiping binge and your curtains, tea towels and domestic pets were infected?

* What if you became the first girl in recorded history to catch crabs by repeatedly listening to Prince's *Purple Rain* album?

Girls in the 1980s tried to learn about sex through the media, but options were limited. The most erotic thing on Irish television at the time was J. R. Ewing sitting up in bed beside a lady large of hair and breast, drinking a glass of bourbon and laughing like a maniac over the downfall of his current nemesis.

Song lyrics were another avenue to be explored. There was a lot of suggestive panting and screeching on the *Bat Out of Hell* album, but the sex was only ever insinuated. And what 80s' child didn't find AC/DC's lyrics suspect? There were sneaking suspicions that 'Giving the Dog a Bone' had very little to do with feeding your pet. Today's lyrics are less subtle. Take Dr. Dre's song 'Bitches ain't Shit', for example, where the good doctor intimates that 'Bitches ain't shit but hoes and tricks, Lick on these nuts and suck the dick'. His medical training has obviously desensitised him.

More often than not, once the 80s' Irish girl had embarked on actual physical contact, she was not very sexually adventurous. Snogging was perfectly acceptable, and the odd grope of a boob, but anything else was taboo. Everything was conducted through the medium of a woolly jumper; at no time was there any flesh-on-flesh contact. In fact, the woolly jumper was symbolic of virtuosity, the Irish equivalent of a burka.

Time passed. Human nature promotes progression, and so arse feeling and a bit of grinding became acceptable. More time passed, and the grinding became more insistent. The Irish girl had crossed over into the Dry Ride Zone. With dry riding you could literally go through the motions without any penetration. Both your reputation and your hymen remained intact, the additional bonus being that you didn't have to look at, or God forbid touch, any unsightly appendages.

Irish girls weren't above a bit of prudish condescension and firmly believed that foreign girls of the same age were far more promiscuous. Apparently American teenagers were going to second or even third base with their boyfriends. Of course, no one had any idea what that actually meant, but it sounded sexually advanced. Thus, the conclusion was drawn that our counterparts in the USA divided their time between cheerleading and choking the chicken, both pastimes being equally incomprehensible as far as your average Irish girl was concerned. Once these American teenagers grew up, it was rumoured that they advanced their sexual experience by becoming groupies for soft rock bands like Journey and Foreigner. As they were not very sexually liberated, Irish women made rubbish groupies by comparison. The boys in Aerosmith were always disappointed with a snog and a dry ride backstage after their Irish shows. For the

Irish girls, getting the bike and the Golden Pages past backstage security was a logistical nightmare.

During the 80s it didn't actually matter how rebellious we were, how many cigarettes we smoked or how much stolen vodka we drank, we were still clueless virgins. So, for the most part, the Catholic dogma worked. Having rebelled against the nuns and everything they represented, a large percentage of the 80s generation remained sexually inexperienced until their twenties. Some even saved themselves for their wedding night. Of course, all of this is laughable now. It's like telling the youth of today that we only had one television channel or that Pac-Man was a revolutionary game with groundbreaking graphics.

⚡ The Walk of Shame ⚡

Nowadays, a night of heavy drinking often results in a one-night stand. There are practical consequences of these actions, namely how to transport yourself to the safety of your home the following morning without being spotted. Is it possible to execute a dignified Walk of Shame? Should it be renamed the Stride of Pride, or will Catholic compunction prevail?

So, can an Irish girl hold her head high and stride confidently when it is blatantly obvious that she has just had sex with a random stranger? The fact that staggering home after a drunken shag has been given such a moniker says a lot about sexuality in Ireland today. Young children on the way to Mass become animated at the spectacle, they point and shout from the back of the car, 'Mummy, Daddy, look, it's the Walk of Shame'. And there you are, a modern-day Mary Magdalene in your skinny jeans and your brand new wedges careening up the road on a wet Sunday morning. Because the Walk of Shame invariably occurs on a Sunday morning, and is an occasion on which the sun rarely shines.

Be that as it may, there are other more urgent issues to be addressed. Firstly, you will have absolutely no fucking idea where you are and will have just spent half an hour trying to find your way out of whichever hellish housing estate you woke up in. Secondly, you will be in a certain amount of physical discomfort. In no particular order, you will be suffering from the following:

* A hangover of epic proportions, which includes a screaming headache, incessant dry retching, and a mouth like Gandhi's sandal.

* As a result of leaping about for hours in the new wedges – Gangnam style – your feet will now resemble bloody stumps. No amount of Compeeds

are going to fix those babies. We are talking foot transplants here.

* You will have at least one orifice that is raw and throbbing.

On a less serious note, your skin will be spotty, your hair matted, and you will bear an uncanny resemblance to Alice Cooper due to the remnants of the previous night's eye make-up. There will be approximately €3 in shrapnel in your purse and your smartphone's battery will have died sometime during the revelry. All of this can be dealt with; it's nothing that a couple of baby wipes and the number 14 bus can't sort out. The real problem here is dealing with the inevitable Catholic guilt.

No matter how many times you try to convince yourself that you are fabulous, an independent woman exploring her sexuality, there will always be that taunting voice whispering the word 'slapper' in your ear. A little incubus or physical manifestation of Catholic guilt (you know the one, looks like Gollum but dresses in a nun's habit) surfaces at this point in time. It sat in the front seat of the Ford Fiesta the night you lost your virginity. It audibly sobbed during your first blow job. And no walk of shame would be complete without this ubiquitous incubus trotting along beside you. Resistance is futile; it's easier just to take its hand and pray that it's familiar with the local bus route. But fear not, the days of the incubus are numbered. The youth of today are unperturbed by notions of chastity.

As the incubus feeds off feelings of self-loathing and monumental shame, its role is redundant among the new generation of Irish girls in present-day Ireland. If confronted by this horrific embodiment, today's youth wouldn't even hesitate before grabbing it, assuming the default duck-mouthed pout, and taking a selfie.

⚡ Online Dating ⚡

As a nation, Ireland is still reluctant to fully embrace the convention of online dating. It wasn't that long ago that we laughed unkindly at desperate Americans looking for love electronically. With the country full of pubs and GAA clubs, why would anyone be reduced to using this outlandish method of meeting their intended? The stigma is waning and, more and more, Irish women are logging on and signing up. Not only are they hooking up with potential soulmates online, but they are also arranging to meet them during the day, in cafés, sober! This is, by far, the most outrageous part of the endeavour. The idea that an Irish woman would ever go on a date, in broad daylight, without two bottles of red wine and a gin and tonic in her to calm the nerves shows the staggering sociological change in this country. However, the geographical limitations of this island are such that anyone who uploads their profile to an online dating website will no sooner have clicked on the 'Submit' button than all their friends, co-workers and former schoolmates will know about it.

If you consider the process of selecting a potential date based on their online dating profile to be a waste of time, and have no compulsion to immerse yourself in the whole 'he isn't one bit attractive but I could grow to love him based on shared interests' justification, then Tinder is the app for you. You can download it at the click of a smartphone button, and it uses your phone's GPS to track down other singles in your area. It's a game in which you quickly rate faces as hot or not, with a swipe of your finger to either the right as a potential hook-up or to the left to consign them to the rejection pile. It's crass, shallow and free, and the prize you get at the end of it? A real-life organic date, with a real-life person.

Tinder encourages the use of your imagination, as you have to visualise what the person really looks like. If you take their profile photo to be a reflection of them at their 100% most attractive with soft focus and flattering filters, then mentally remove the filter, sharpen their features, add approximately five years and two stone in weight and throw in some blemishes. If you still like what you see, then it's a swipe to the right for this Adonis.

In Ireland there is a huge risk that you will end up dating your second cousin. Having survived the famine, internment, the 80s' recession and Garthgate, a single Irish woman still finds herself living on a small island with a male:female ratio of 1:3. The awful reality is that, should she best the other two women in the cut-throat contest for that elusive, charming Irish rogue, the chances are he will probably end up being related to her.

While all of this online dating sounds like a thrilling pastime, it is a bit exclusionary for Irish women who have already snagged their Irish boy-wonder. With a slight modification to their app, the Tinder organisation could provide some dual functionality with the introduction of Ginder. By downloading the Ginder version of the app, an Irish woman need never worry about where her next gin and tonic is coming from. She can configure the distance setting to a five-kilometre radius and sit back, comforted in the knowledge that no matter where the funeral or under-sevens GAA match is located, she is always within reach of staple solace in the form of quinine and alcohol.

*

There have been major changes in Irish societal norms regarding intimate and sexual relationships. The approach towards sex and sexuality is becoming progressively more liberal, and although some of the older generation may accuse modern-day Irish girls of having questionable sexual mores, there is no doubt that there have been many positive developments. Access to professional sexual health services that has led to the demystification of the crabs myths. Maybe young Irish girls are increasingly engaging in the Walk of Shame, but at least they are practising safe sex, and the stigma associated with unwanted pregnancies has waned in the past ten years. The practice of hedging may not be symbolic of the advancement of humanity, but Ireland passing the referendum on same-sex marriage most certainly is.

5.

The Queen of Quirky

Traits Unique to Irish Women

What do you get if you cross the life and soul of the party with an insecure people-pleaser? An Irish woman, of course! We are a mass of contradictions. For the most part, we are genuinely uncomfortable receiving compliments. On the other hand, the mere hint of a slight or insult turns an Irish woman into a snarling she-devil. We never complain in restaurants and avoid confrontation at all costs. Yet our favourite pastime is complete character assassination.

There are a number of explanations for this phenomenon. Firstly, having been born lacking in the looks department (see Chapter 3), we have compensated by developing massive personalities. It's a well-known fact that Irish men are intimidated by stunners. They are happier with a woman who laughs uproariously at their jokes and knocks back pints of Guinness all night. We aspire to being one of the lads, and what better way to achieve this than to utilise the word 'fuckin' as a one-size-fits-all adjective and adverb.

An Irish woman will arrive into the pub on any given night and announce loudly that 'It's fuckin' freezin' out' and that she'd 'murder a fuckin' pint'. With those two sentences she will have caught the attention of every Irish male in the vicinity. As the night progresses, our heroine is seen to have the time of her life as she works the room like a society hostess with Tourette's. As the level of inebriation increases, so do her charms. By closing time, her peals of laughter are accompanied by the fail-safe knee-slapping routine. She may not be the best-looking woman they've ever seen, but at least 70% of the Irish men in the pub want to marry her at that point.

⋀ Massive Personalities ⋀

Irish people love to laugh and, by that rationale, they love people who make them laugh. We will forgive many things, but having no sense of humour is considered a cardinal sin. Adulterers, thieves, bankers, lying scumbags, crooked politicians – it doesn't matter how serious the offence is – they can expect nothing less than immediate absolution as long as they are brilliant craic.

Most massive personalities are generated from a very young age. Traditional Irish families were large, and an average-sized family in the 80s had in excess of seven children. Parents were busy and attention was scarce, and so it was important to establish yourself as a 'character', thereby guaranteeing a disproportionate share of your parents' affection. If that didn't work, you were reduced to bed-wetting.

A guaranteed way to become the most celebrated child in an Irish family is to start swearing at a very young age. If an Irish child has reached the age of three and has not yet told someone to 'fuck off', there will be a certain amount of familial concern. The inoffensive child may be brought for a hearing test or even a developmental check. There will be huge relief all around when eventually the slow starter calls Granny 'a bollox'. Everyone will fall around laughing, delighted with the child. The child's mother will proudly relate the story to her friends and colleagues. All of this will have taught the youngster two valuable lessons about being Irish: firstly, a lack of vocabulary is easily remedied by cursing, and secondly, as long as you can make people laugh, you will be loved by everybody in Ireland.

School years were spent perfecting the massive personality. This was especially useful if you found yourself in the home economics class when certain other girls were learning Honours French. Being the class clown was an excellent antidote to education and ensured enormous kudos. Constant swearing and the ability to blow perfect smoke rings at the back of the bicycle shed were mandatory skills. Performing well in school was something that only gobshites did – everything was secondary to being the life and soul of the party. Homework and studying were unnecessary evils, and little thought was given to how this might affect her choice of profession. Any discussions in the 80s regarding an Irish schoolgirl's future took place during Career Guidance, which was delivered at one sitting by an elderly nun. Girls were presented with three life choices: become a nun, a teacher or a nurse. Attending college was something you did to facilitate becoming a teacher. Any other course of study was considered pure affectation. But all of this was immaterial; you had no career concerns because you were brilliant craic. Everyone knew that this skill would ensure that you sailed through life. No one would ever be able to resist your Irish charms, and this would bring the requisite fame and fortune.

⚡ Comfortable Silence ⚡

However, even hilarious Irish women have their off days. Once you have been labelled as brilliant craic, it is a hard persona to shake off. Never again will you be allowed a break from talking. The phrase 'comfortable silence' is considered to be a contradiction in terms. It is said that nature abhors a vacuum – empty or unfilled spaces are unnatural as they go against the laws of physics. This is nothing compared to the way an Irish woman views a pause in conversation. A spell of silence defies her laws of nature, and she is compelled by a force greater than herself to fill that silence. The fact that she may have nothing worthwhile to say is immaterial. Who among us has not been guilty of verbal diarrhoea or the small talk scutters?

In particular, many Irish women love to perform running commentaries on the passing landscape during lengthy car journeys. You will probably be familiar with the likes of: 'Look at the trees, there's a big house, cows, the state of these roads, more cows….' It's like I Spy, minus the subterfuge.

Rapid-firing machine-gun speech is required to deal with those unnatural types (probably non-Irish) who are perfectly at ease with a lull in conversation. Popular topics include detailing everything you have had to eat that day, or listing all the people you know who have recently been diagnosed with cancer. Whatever it takes, the silence must be filled quickly and completely.

Another related trait in an Irish woman is their propensity to exaggerate. Every single Irish woman in the world exaggerates, all the time. Their numerical accounts are especially not to be trusted. If they were delayed by ten minutes in traffic, they will recount their horrific two-hour ordeal. If asked how many people were in attendance at an event, they will always say thirty-seven, no matter how grossly exaggerated this figure is. There is a good reason why you don't know any Irish female accountants. Also, an Irish woman is never a little bit hungry, thirsty or hungover. An Irish woman is always DYING from the aforementioned conditions. Although we are prone to bigging things up, however, this never applies to our own merits.

⚡ Aversion to Compliments ⚡

Recent sociological experiments carried out at Athlone Institute of Technology have proven, once and for all, that Irish women have a genetic aversion to compliments. A voice-over artist was hired to narrate a number of audio compliment recordings, thereafter known as the 'Grand Cake, Nora' series. A cross section of Irish females were restrained then subjected to the recordings, played in a loop with ever-increasing levels of volume. Scientists proceeded to study the reactions of the women. Initially, the recordings appeared to have little or no effect. The women could be seen to accept the compliments with a slight incline of the head and some gracious murmurings. Before long, however, the women's discomfort manifested itself. They began shifting in their seats and the occasional facial tic was observed. After approximately three hours of intense flattery, some of the women broke down and wept. Others reacted with violent outbursts. 'Sure look at the state of me' and 'My house smells like shite' were just some of the denials that can be read in the transcript log. The experiment was supposed to be conducted over a period of five days, but it had to be stopped after just one day as the extreme stress and anxiety experienced by the Irish women was deemed detrimental to their long-term health.

So why do Irish women find flattery that abhorrent? Is our self-esteem so low that we cannot imagine anyone being appreciative of our looks? Maybe it is because Irish men are not prone to lavish praise. Consequently, we are unpractised in the art of graciously accepting a compliment. It is therefore inadvisable for Irish women to have relationships with French men. They cannot curb their natural obsequiousness and, sadly, the Irish woman will find his gallantry nauseating in the extreme. It will all end in tears (probably his) as his little Irish *fleur* will eventually announce that he has her head wrecked and that she is off to find herself the perfect Irish man – preferably one who will take her for granted and make insensitive comments about the size of her arse.

This affliction is so ingrained that we cannot even receive compliments from other Irish women. Even an innocuous situation where a friend remarks 'I like your top' can cause consternation. You would think that any woman would be pleased to be admired by her peers. *Au contraire*, the average Irish woman will react in one of three ways:

* Rebuff the compliment by belittling the item under discussion, e.g. 'Oh, this old rag? I've had it for years' or 'Thanks, Penneys' best.'

* Immediately draw attention to a perceived failing: 'Yes, but have you seen the size of my arse?' or 'Look! I have psoriasis all over my elbows.'

* Parry the compliment with a return compliment, thereby making them feel uncomfortable. Better still, introduce a bit of paranoia into the equation,

such as 'I was just saying to Mary the other day how well you are looking'. Firstly, this lets them know that yourself and Mary had a rendezvous to which they were not invited, and secondly that they were the main topic of conversation.

⋏ People-Pleasing ⋏

It is ironic, considering an Irish woman's inability to give negative feedback to anyone, that beneath this considerate exterior is the desperate desire to make everyone love us. How many of us have sat in a restaurant, gazing miserably at our overpriced and inedible meal, and then, when the waitress asks if everything is okay, we answer that the food was delicious but we just are not that hungry? Rather than being furious at the poor quality of the meal, we are ultimately relieved that we have avoided confrontation. Whether she is eating in a restaurant or speaking to the consultant who has just made a critical error during her life-saving surgery ('I didn't like to bother the nice doctor, I'm sure one lung looks very like much like another') the most important consideration for the Irish woman will be not to make a fuss.

Similarly, in many countries a trip to the hairdresser is considered to be a treat for a woman – a nice way to relax, read a few *Hello* magazines and get your hair looking fabulous all at once. Why then is an appointment in your average Irish hair salon such a soul-destroying experience? Upon your arrival, the receptionist will give your outfit a condescending up and down glance that leaves you in no doubt that your jeans are not skinny enough and your new top is something her granny wouldn't be seen dead in. Then, no matter how much effort you have made with your afflicted hair and make-up that morning, the minute you sit in front of the enormous mirror and study your reflection under the Guantanamo Bay type lighting, you will look hideous.

Your stylist will bound over to you and the short battle of wills commences as you try to assert your authority and dissuade her from trying something more funky and modern this time. You will repeatedly beg her just to give your hair a trim and leave the length, but to no avail. As we all know, Irish hairdressers will do exactly what they want to do to your hair. More often than not, they will attempt to recreate the latest look that *all* the celebrities are sporting. They are oblivious to the fact that you do not have eyes like Mila Kunis or cheekbones like Jennifer Garner. Inevitably, they will win the battle and after two hours of lukewarm coffee and inane chit-chat, you gaze in horror at your feathery, elfin style. Your stylist will skip off to get a hand mirror so you can see the back of your head, which will have been styled in the manner of Kim Kardashian's buttocks.

This is all regrettable, but what is absolutely scarring about the whole experience is that an Irish woman will announce to everyone in the salon that she absolutely LOVES her new look, leave a generous tip, walk outside and promptly burst into tears.

⚡ Begrudgery ⚡

A less endearing personality trait that is specific to Irish women is their innate ability to begrudge. We only like people when they are down and out. In Ireland we love a lame duck, and you will never receive as much care and support as when you have fallen on hard times. Once people start to get back on their feet, their support network will rapidly dwindle. If they are lucky enough to haul themselves out of the doldrums and achieve some relative success, they will be viewed with suspicion. The hypothesis is that successful people in Ireland are actively disliked. The animosity felt towards an individual increases in proportion to their wealth and prosperity.

The nation's attitude towards Bono is a good example of this. Whenever U2 were an up-and-coming rock band, slogging it out in shitty venues across the country, they were national heroes, northside Dubs made good. Every man, woman and child in Ireland owned the *Boy*, *October* and *War* albums and knew all the words to all the songs. A couple of years later, U2 were gaining notoriety abroad and, collectively, the Irish population started to resent this popularity. By the time *Rattle and Hum* came out, they were viewed with a certain amount of disdain. Then it emerged that three out of the four band members had moved to the south side of Dublin city. This was viewed as the ultimate sell-out, equally as loathsome as Iggy Pop, the godfather of punk, selling car insurance.

Today, Bono is considered to be one of the biggest wankers this country has ever produced, and he literally cannot give away his latest album. All he has to do is bound onto a stage sporting his shades and his leather trousers and the entire Irish race vomits in unison. It doesn't matter what he does; he will never regain the national pride and affection he held before he became famous. If he saves billions of African lives or manages single-handedly to cancel Third World debt, it will only serve to increase his lack of popularity at home. There is also a little-known clause in the

Irish Constitution relating to the wearing of leather trousers. It states that Irish law forbids the wearing of these trousers and actively enforces discrimination on these grounds.

⚡ Extreme Slander ⚡

The Jekyll to our people-pleasing Hyde is an Irish woman's fixation with gossip. Gossiping is a national pastime practised by all Irish females, young and old. Ranging from how-ya's to the upper echelons of society, gossiping transcends class barriers. Some nationalities have a penchant for skiing or mountain biking; we practise extreme slander. If knowledge is power, then salacious insight is currency in this country. Grown women have been known to beg for a mere morsel of gossip. A good juicy cut of gossip is something to be savoured, and it is important not to rush the telling of the tale.

Many Irish women will commence with an introduction to the subject in question, who they are and where they come from. They will start with a brief look at the family tree outlining who the person's parents were and what they did for a living. Any previous transgressions or history of scandal in the family will be referred to. This insinuates that the storyteller had already predicted the occurrence of the misdeed.

Some feel obliged to pinpoint the exact geographical location where the offender resides. You will probably not be listening to a word they are saying, but the teller of the tale may become irritated if they sense your lack of interest and, God forbid, they might withhold the gossip as a result of your insincerity. It is therefore important to pretend you know exactly which townland they are referring to, where the local shop is, the second turn on the right and the house with the sash windows. Finally, having dragged the proverbial arse out of it, they will announce that the person in question has been expelled, fired, impregnated or cuckolded. The correct response is 'OH MY GOD! I DON'T BELIEVE IT!' Alternatively, there is always 'Shut. Up.' or 'Fuck. Off.' said very slowly and clearly to indicate extreme surprise.

Once you have been the recipient of a titbit of gossip, you need to think very carefully about what to do with this precious gift. An Irish woman who has been sworn to secrecy is like a ticking time bomb. She is liable to incur internal injuries if she does not get to transmit her secret rapidly and completely. So, exactly how many people can an Irish woman tell when she has been 'sworn to secrecy'?

It's best to limit your gossiping to your best friend and one other randomly selected friend. Telling your partner is hardly worthwhile. Most men have an unsophisticated memory process not unlike an Etch A Sketch. You can spend an hour and a half setting the scene and recounting the most riveting scandal of the decade, then, upon offering him a cup of tea, every single word you have just uttered will be erased from his memory forever. Colleagues don't really count either as they exist in a parallel universe; if there's a lull in conversation at the water dispenser, knock yourself out.

Another risk is that you may be overheard, and as we all know, there are only three degrees of separation in Ireland. It has been mathematically proven that everyone in Ireland is connected by their cousin's boyfriend's friend. The secret may be at risk of spreading exponentially when an Irish woman is sworn to secrecy. As time passes, you may forget that it was ever a secret in the first place. This is a dangerous period as you could inadvertently post the news on Facebook, and people can be quite touchy and overly sensitive about this sort of thing – fucking Luddites.

There are those that consider being entrusted with a secret to be a massive burden. The Fellowship of the Ring has nothing on it. Stopping an Irish woman mid sentence and saying, 'Well, if it's such a big secret then maybe it's best not to tell me' is guaranteed to piss her off on a number of different levels:

* You are displaying signs of being 'no craic' and, as outlined previously, this is majorly frowned upon.

* You are being holier than thou, which casts them in a bad light – another no-no.

* They now have to find someone else to tell, a more appreciative audience.

* Any conversations conducted afterwards will be mind-numbingly boring for both of you.

This refusal may, in fact, jeopardise your friendship forever, so it's best to get a nice cup of tea and some Kimberley biscuits, then lean in and assume the globally accepted expression of utter surprise by widening your eyes and dropping open your lower jaw.

⚡ Tag Gossiping ⚡

Occasionally, there is an incumbent responsibility associated with the secret. Usually it will be about a friend or acquaintance whose partner is cheating on them. The gossiper is forcing you, the gossipee, to make a moral choice on whether you blow the lid on the whole thing. It is a sort of tag gossiping. They tell you, then 'you're it' and the original secret-bearer is absolved. It's a sly enough manoeuvre, most likely undertaken by an Irish Bitch in the true sense of the word. Industry advice says to keep your mouth shut. Relationships will come and go, but in all probability they will probably get back with the two-timing bastard. They will even forgive the girl who was sleeping with their fella before the messenger will be exonerated. Finally, they will reserve a special little corner of hatred in their hearts for the smug wagon that couldn't wait to break the news.

⚡ Performing Monkeys ⚡

Most of the aforementioned personality traits are specific to Irish women. European girls don't partake in any discernible people-pleasing and seem to be quite happy to sit in silence for hours at a time. Occasionally, when asked a direct question, they may shrug or even sneer. They don't appear to have any manic compulsion to make everyone like them in fact, they couldn't actually give a shit if you like them or not. Their self-assuredness is awe-inducing and their detached demeanour makes a mockery of everything an Irish woman stands for. Many Irish women default to performing monkey mode when they find themselves in the company of a number of female foreigners. If the Irish woman is unable to generate a bit of craic, or even the occasional verbal response, she will often up the ante out of desperation. In the more extreme cases, she may even resort to full-blown Andrew Lloyd Webber tactics, performing a solo re-enactment of the entire *Cats* musical in the canteen at work under the cool appraising gaze of her foreign co-workers.

To add insult to injury, many of these women are naturally beautiful with sallow skin and thick, luxurious hair. The only saving grace is that on a night out some of them dress like Eurovision backing vocalists, which is obviously a huge relief to our Irish lass. Now, due to the fact that we are no longer ugly, the Irish woman can hold her own beside these fabulous foreigners and is freed from her larger than life personality shackles. There is no need for us to be hilarious, the life and soul of the party and one of the lads all rolled into one. Characters, stand down. Let's take our recently paid for good looks and use them to become mysterious, or better still, aloof.

If you, too, are tired of being an Irish woman, why don't you take a minibreak and adopt a contra personality. The following are some pointers to assist you in becoming Gretchen, Olga, Annika or Aurélie:

* Cycle everywhere.

* Complain loudly in restaurants.

* Stop smiling at complete strangers.

* Start carrying around books about philosophers (can be transported in basket on front of bicycle).

* Only drink Perrier in pubs and never buy a round.

* Wear loose, flowing clothing and create the illusion of height by standing up straight.

* Only speak when spoken to, and make sure that when you do finally speak that you say something profound.

* Pretend to be very open sexually, maybe even snog a few women.

After one week of the aforementioned behaviour, you will welcome a dose of verbal diarrhoea and some hard-core people-pleasing.

6.

The Demon Drink

Alcohol, Catholic Sacraments and Boozy Bulimia

Much has been made of the Irish nation's fondness for the occasional social beverage, and recent polls have indicated that 16% of young Irish women are binge drinking on a weekly basis. Twice as many fights and accidents occur amongst Irish female drinkers than in other countries. Some might argue that these statistics are alarmist. As we all know, Irish people only go to the pub to get away from the inclement weather. By that rationale, the other countries involved in the poll must either have great weather or shite pubs. Perhaps these countries are populated with people who are absolutely no craic at all and their pubs are to be avoided?

This poses the question: when does the craic end and full-blown alcoholism begin? This distinction has traditionally been somewhat blurred for Irish men, and the aforementioned statistics indicate that it is becoming increasingly blurred for Irish women too.

As there is a thin line between heavy drinking and raving alcoholism, it is necessary to pigeonhole your drinking habits, thereby distracting your family and friends from the reality of the situation. A relatively new term that Irish women like to bandy about is that of the 'social drinker', which makes it sound like you spend your nights drinking Martinis and eating Ferrero Rochers at the Ambassador's Residence. There is always the possibility that the entire population of Ireland are simply functioning alcoholics. Perhaps Shirley MacLaine's character in the movie *Postcards from the Edge* hit the nail on the head when she stated: 'I am not an alcoholic; I just drink like an Irish person'.

⚡ Drunken Behaviour Checklist ⚡

The first step of the mystical twelve-step programme practised by people in recovery is to admit that they are powerless in the face of alcohol or that the demon drink has taken over their lives. Surely this is a subjective statement, and what constitutes this dependency varies from nation to nation and from person to person? It is also a given that people must have reached a low point in their lives before they can begin to climb back up from the depths of despair in which they find themselves. Usually they drink for a number of years then cross an invisible line that makes them realise that they have a problem and subsequently seek help with that problem. Many Irish women have trouble identifying that line.

The following Drunken Behaviour checklist is equal parts hen party icebreaker and alcohol dependency identifier. Many of the below activities are considered to be quite normal for Irish girls and would never raise alarm bells or prompt the googling of their nearest AA meeting. Why not invite your friends round and complete the questionnaire over a bottle or two of vino and a bucket of Doritos?

Have you ever:

* Smuggled cheap alcohol into a venue by hiding it about your person 'Crouching Tiger, Hidden Naggin' style?

* Squatted on the street and pissed in public?

* Drank heavily for a number of hours, vomited in the toilet then continued to drink in a rejuvenated

state for the rest of the night? This is termed Boozy Bulimia or Boozlemia for short.

* Fallen asleep in a pub or nightclub?

* Fallen asleep and/or vomited during sex?

* Woken up in the morning with your head in a kebab?

* Puked into your handbag during the taxi ride home?

* Sexually harassed your boss and/or simulated lewd sexual acts on the dance floor during the office Christmas party?

This exercise can be enhanced by adding some personal favourites. Feel free to extend the list with some of your own unique drunken anecdotes, such as falling asleep under a parked motorcycle or waking up after a night of heavy drinking with chewing gum stuck in your pubic hair. If you present this list to most Irish women, they will admit to having performed at least one of these acts and qualify this bizarre behaviour with the one size fits all excuse: 'Sure I was locked!'

At least part of the problem seems to be our inability to know when to call it a night. We should take it as a given that once a gal is more concerned with masking her body odours than fixing her hair, she should throw in the towel. So why are Irish girls unable to go out, have a couple of drinks and just go home? The primary reason seems to that we are petrified of missing out on the craic. Having mighty craic is more important than dignity, sanity or retaining your employment. FOMO or Fear of Missing Out is a new phenomenon for the social media generation, and most young Irish women live in this perpetual state of anxiety. Now, thanks to Snapchat, you can witness first-hand the life-changing, amazingly brilliant night that everyone is having without you. No matter how embarrassed or fuckin' morto an Irish woman is the day-after-the-night-before, they feel compelled to tell everyone they know about their actions and present their technicolour account of it to the wider world. Rather than being ashamed by our behaviour as a result of excessive drinking, Irish women are uncommonly proud of it. It is said that Irish people will sneak into their local AA meeting, petrified of being seen, but have no problem falling out onto the road in a pathetic heap of drunken misery at closing time.

⋏ Drinking and Catholic Sacraments ⋏

Irish girls usually start drinking at around thirteen years of age. Having just received the Holy Spirit during the sacrament of Confirmation, they embark on a life-long relationship with a much more invigorating spirit.

Baptism

These same girls spent the day of their Baptism surrounded by alcohol, although they were oblivious to the fact. The modern-day Catholic ritual for the Baptism of a child involves an old-fashioned ceremony where the priest asks the parents and godparents a series of questions, including the following:

> Priest: Do you reject Satan, father of sin and prince of darkness (to give him his full title)?
> Parents and Godparents: I do.
> Priest: Do you reject the glamour of evil, and refuse to be mastered by sin?
> Parents and Godparents: I do.
> (Author aside: the glamour of evil sounds very enticing though, and I, for one, would be sorry if I never got to be mastered by sin, but apparently you have to stick to the script and 'Can I get back to you on the glamour clause?' just doesn't cut it.)

No one finds it even slightly ironic that the aforementioned Spanish Inquisition is promptly followed by a dash to the designated venue to start the drinking session. At 10 a.m. the congregation is solemnly ensconced in the middle of a full-blown exorcism. By 11.30 a.m. attendees are reclining in a leather armchair in the nearest hotel lobby nursing the first bevy of the day. Both the prince of darkness and the new born baby are all but forgotten.

Communion

The Holy Communion ceremony lacks the gravitas of the Baptism, and there is little or no mention of Satan, vampires or indeed any members of the undead. Clearly this is another sacrament that necessitates a piss-up. What better way to celebrate all those little girls becoming Christ's brides than for their family members, neighbours and close family friends to get systematically plastered. The girls in question are more concerned with mentally calculating the number of Kit Kats they can purchase with the fat roll of fifty euro notes that is now wedged into their white diamonté clutch purses. They may notice as the day progresses that all their aunts and uncles seem to be talking loudly and saying the work 'fuck' a lot, but it matters not, so long as the Fanta and Tayto Cheese & Onion keep rolling in.

Confirmation

The last childhood sacrament undertaken by Irish Catholics is the Confirmation ceremony. This is considered to be a right of passage. The Irish girl is now twelve or thirteen years old, and is coming of age. She has achieved a certain level of independence and is allowed to choose her own Confirmation name, but only if it is the name of a saint, a biblical character or that of the local postmistress. With this new-found freedom comes a natural curiosity. She begins to wonder what the big attraction is with drinking and, as luck would have it, puberty is kicking in at the same time. This is a potentially disastrous situation.

The Catholic Church are no fools; they know what teenagers are like and so they did what any self-respecting authoritarian regime would do and came up with The Pledge. The Pledge is a vow that is taken as part of the ritual of Confirmation, where the young adult commits to abstaining from alcohol until they are at least eighteen years old. The Catholic Church tries to sneak The Pledge past distracted teenagers, unnoticed, like the Irish Government does with referendums. In fact, there are other similarities with Irish voting practices as the vow is not verbalised, it is made in silence. Only the teenager, their conscience and God are privy to the deal. Expecting a teenager to make the correct ethical decision based on their intrinsic morality is like giving chocolate to a toddler and stipulating that they mustn't eat it until after their dinner. Chances are, you will be disappointed with the outcome.

Most teenagers who bow to authoritative pressure and take The Pledge are prone to break this morally binding contract within just a couple of months. This action proves to be a more telling rite of passage for them than the sacrament of Confirmation itself. It introduces them to the anarchic, half-arsed approach that the Irish nation has towards some of its laws. (Irish women, in particular, are partial to lawbreaking on a regular basis. Some of the laws they regularly flout include: the drink driving law, the learner drivers having a full licence holder in the car with them at all times law, the television licence law, the drug possession law (e.g. purchasing Solpadeine abroad and muling it into Ireland), the using a mobile phone while driving law, the defamation, libel and slander laws, and perhaps the most commonly broken, the blasphemy law.)

Marriage

Before you know it, our heroine is walking up the aisle to receive the sacrament of Marriage. On the morning of the wedding, as she is getting her hair and make-up done, it is customary to drink a bottle or two of champagne. The champers gives rise to a short period of elation and excitement that is superseded by the Bridezilla phase, which unfortunately lasts for the remainder of the day/year/marriage. During the course of this particular day, the combination of tension and alcohol will cause the bride to:

* Become hysterical over a misplaced eyelash.

* Scream abuse at her bridesmaids for not anticipating her every whim.

* Completely ignore her new husband with the exception of the first dance, where they both pretend to converse through tortured fake smiles.

* Recoil in horror at the vision of her friends dirty dancing with her uncle, Noel.

Upon arrival at the wedding reception, all the wedding guests look neat and well groomed. But within a couple of hours they will start to fray around the edges; by 8 p.m. there are ladders in tights, and by 10 p.m. most women are dancing in their bare feet, and previously tucked in articles of clothing have come loose. By midnight, all upstyles have collapsed, shoes will be missing, lipstick is smudged and false eyelashes are randomly dispersed among the body's crevices like some previously undiscovered Amazonian parasite. The physical degeneration is hardly surprising when you consider that by the time the evening's entertainment draws to a close, most people have drunk their own body weight in a combination of beers, wines and spirits.

So, for all the key events in an Irish Catholic girl's life, the celebration is inextricably linked to alcohol. However, there are some other defining moments that should be celebrated and are often overlooked. A child's first day at school is the perfect opportunity for a party as the house is suddenly free of children. Why not organise a piss-up in your home and invite other mothers whose children have also commenced national school in the area? The most appropriate drink for this occasion would be gin and tonic. As there is little or no smell from a G & T, the chances of the junior infants' teacher getting suspicious are minimal.

During the pre-Xanax age and in the absence of any decent anti-depressants in Ireland, the G & T was the widely accepted 'mother's little helper' and supported many Irish Mammies through post-natal depression, bad marriages and the 80s' recession.

⚡ The Long March Home ⚡

Most Irish girls begin their alcohol consumption with stealing booze from their parents' drinks cabinet. The standard drinks cabinet in Ireland contains bottles of whiskey, gin, vodka, Baileys, brandy (for medicinal purposes) and one expensive bottle of red wine that no one is ever allowed to drink. The girls usually decant a selection of stolen liquor and mix it all together in one plastic bottle. They stash this under their jackets and head off with a couple of friends to find a suitable spot for their underage drinking exploits. The only way it is physically possible for someone to drink the stolen concoction is to simultaneously pinch their nose to deaden the taste and knock it back. Once most of the assembled party are slurring their words and stumbling about, adopting the globally accepted standard demeanour of a drunk person, it is up to the one sensible (boring) girl present to half drag, half carry her companions back home from the designated field or bus shelter.

Instead of being grateful for this support, her pissed friends are alternating between screaming abuse at her and hugging her and telling her how much they love her.

They eventually collapse en masse in a sobbing, vomiting heap. Anyone in their right mind would abandon them and be home in time for *The X-Factor*, but Irish girls love a bit of drama. The reliable friend is tasked with removing all traces of mud and vomit from her buddies and sobering them up before returning them to their various homes. The detox consists of countless cups of coffee and a series of sharp slaps about their faces, which has the combined effect of sobering them up and getting revenge for subjecting her to the Irish teenage equivalent of the Long March Home.

Once these teenage girls are allowed to attend discos, their drink of choice becomes slightly more sophisticated. As they still cannot get served in pubs, they have to harass passers-by to purchase their naggin of vodka for them. It is important that they choose their personal shopper carefully to reduce the risk of being brought home by the gardaí. Targeting males aged between twenty and forty who look like they, too, are about to commence a night's drinking is the most sensible approach. Unsurprisingly, the men they approach are not averse to being surrounded by a group of giddy teenage girls who are instantly beholden to them. Once the alcohol has been consumed, the girls stagger around the town towards the disco like newborn gazelles.

The next task is to ensure that every member of the gang of girls is allowed into the venue. Everyone will be scrutinised by the doorman and the box office lady on the way in for potential insurance risks. If one of the assembled girls is paralytic, the recommended manoeuvre is to have one girl positioned on either side of the drunken girl in question and then drape her arms around their shoulders to give the overall impression of camaraderie as opposed to the 'carrying a wounded soldier' look. However, the doorman may notice that her head is lolling in an alarming fashion. On closer inspection, the girl could be found to be unconscious and drooling excessively. No amount of assurances that she is just a little tired due to excessive studying will gain access for the girl at this point.

Then comes the moral dilemma. What is to be done with her? It is common practice to deposit her senseless form on an old trailer or a tractor tyre around the back of the venue and cover her in leaves and branches to conceal her from any potentially predatory males. Her carers can then enter the venue with a self-congratulatory air, the first few bars of 'Uptown Funk' completely eliminating any last vestiges of concern they had for their friend.

⩗ Out on the Town ⩘

Once Irish girls reach the age of eighteen, their drinking practices become much more civilised. They wouldn't dream of dumping a friend on top of disused farm equipment. Let us consider an average night out for an Irish girl who is legally allowed to drink.

Phase 1: The Preparation – no alcohol consumed to date

This is the lengthiest of the six phases. An Irish girl can take up to three days to prepare for a big night out. Fake tan should be applied a minimum of two days in advance. Nails are added on the day prior to the event. Then, finally, there is hair to be straightened or given soft curls and make-up to be applied – including the ominous task of gluing on false eyelashes. The end result must be flawless. Ironically, like the ritualistic destruction of a sand mandala, during the following five phases, all work carried out in Phase 1 is systematically obliterated.

Phase 2: Pre-drinks – number of drinks consumed = 2 or 3

A recent addition to the archetypical stages of a night out is the Pre-drinks or 'Prinks' phase. Prinks involves all the Irish females gathering in someone's house to drink cheap liquor, trowel on more make-up and record the whole event on Snapchat or Instagram. There will always be at least two discernible characters in attendance. The Time Nazi and the Messy Drunk. The Time Nazi is the girl who freaks out because everyone is going to miss the bus or be too late to get into the club. Hers is a thankless task, trying to organise the assembled females without spontaneous combustion from apoplexy. At the very least, she will need a border collie and a taser gun just to get the gang out the door. The Messy Drunk is the girl who gets so plastered during Prinks that she falls asleep and misses the whole night out. This is probably just as well: if the Messy Drunk stays awake long enough to make it out to the pub or the club, the Time Nazi will end up having to mind her all night and will proceed to ruin everyone's buzz by complaining bitterly to anyone that will listen. Due to the incredibly high levels of volume at the Prinks gathering, this is usually only practised by Irish girls before they become mothers. Once you have children, you typically have around seven minutes to get ready for a big night on the town as you have to clean up the crime scene in the kitchen after dinner, express a litre of breast milk and get your offspring to sleep before you can go anywhere. When you have managed to get them to nod off, you will need to levitate down the stairs and out the front door to ensure you don't wake the little angels. Frequently, the new Irish Mammy will end up falling asleep on the floor beside their child's cot, exhausted from the aforementioned dairy transfusion, thereby missing her first night out in a year.

Phase 3: Having the Craic – number of drinks imbibed to date = 5

This is known colloquially as the loosening up phase and usually takes place in a bar or club. During this period, an Irish girl begins to relax and have the craic. The craic usually involves all of the gathered company 'slagging' each other, i.e. subjecting one of their friends to a series of thinly veiled insults that implies that they are of loose morals, stupid, or a combination of both. The only difference between slagging and character assassination is that the slaggee is always present for the verbal onslaught. The slaggers will usually rake up some undesirable ex-boyfriend from the girl's past to kick off the ritual humiliation. When this topic has been exhausted, they will move on to the next girl, who will be subjected to a similar barrage.

Once all females in attendance have been slagged, the only remaining topic of conversation is sex and male sexual organs. As the evening teeters on the cusp of Phase 4, it's wall-to-wall willies, goolies and ridin'. Each reference is following by loud, guttural guffaws. The volume of the conversation has increased by a number of decibels, and there is a lot of knee-slapping and playful shoulder-shoving. There may be the occasional foray onto the dance floor, where all the girls will dance in a circle. Irish girls all utilise the same dance technique. The leg movements consist of a basic stepping from side to side while the hands are busy with a series of unfathomable pointing gestures: pointing up to the ceiling, pointing at the person in front of you and then pointing to the left and to the right with alternate hands. Should the music switch to Beyonce's 'Single Ladies' at any point, the hands will immediately change from random pointing to one hand on the hip and the other performing the infamous hand twirl move.

Phase 4: The Eye of the Storm – total number of drinks quaffed = 8

By Phase 4, you are entering the eye of the storm. The joviality is waning and a slight air of melancholy has permeated the amassed gang of girls. Topics for discussion at this point might include unhappy childhoods, unrequited love and previous slights or arguments amongst the group. At least 50% of the Irish women present will be welling up with tears and a number of them will already be bawling in the toilet. This is standard behaviour for Irish women on a night out and is in no way considered to be a social disaster. *Au contraire*, Phase 4 is a natural progression and leads us seamlessly into Phase 5.

Phase 5: The Repetition Phase – drinks tally for the night = 11

At this point of the night everyone is drinking vodka and whites or gin and tonics. The keyword for this phase is repetition. Its commencement is easily identified as all the Irish girls are reiterating the same point over and over again, the only variation being the increase in volume. In keeping with the mating rituals of wolves, a number of the assembled Irish girls will break away from the pack to mate. Roughly half of the girls will have wandered off and two or three out of the gang will be shifting someone they shouldn't be shifting, such as the aforementioned undesirable ex-boyfriend. In fact, these girls will have their tongues stuck down the throats of people they vehemently swore that they hated with a passion and wouldn't look at in a million years only three hours earlier during Phase 3.

Phase 6: The Hen Party Hat-Trick

This is the most varied of all the phases. The remaining women tend to be either snogging, singing or spewing. A combination of all three is difficult to achieve. At the end of the night, most Irish girls will have lost at least one of the following: her phone, her bag, her coat, her shoes, the ability to walk, her dignity. Once again it is up to the Time Nazi to assemble the original gang, find all the lost property, get everyone out of the club, to the chipper, take their orders, then get them into their various taxis and home. This is the girl most likely to embark upon a career in HR.

⚡ Marketing Alcohol in Ireland ⚡

Being aware of Phases 1–6, the Irish drinks industry is faced with a difficult task. They have to come up with new and exciting ways to package alcohol while simultaneously pretending that:

a)   Alcohol isn't that bad for you.
b)   Irish people do not have a problem with drink.
c)   They actually give a shit about anything other that making shedloads of money.

The Alcohol Beverage Federation of Ireland should get some tips from the US Department of Defence, where they have a long history of sugar-coating the development of products that cause the deaths of millions of civilians. At the moment they are focusing on the future capability of drones, and hope to produce drones that will be able to deviate from mission commands set by humans if they spot a better target. They will hunt in 'swarms', and could be patrolling skies within the next twenty-five years. While this all sounds slightly more sinister than a night on the Jägerbombs, it doesn't detract from the fact that both organisations have a hard time generating a humanitarian public image and raising their brand power. These guys are past masters at marketing under difficult circumstances and Diageo could do worse than picking up the phone and getting some friendly advice from Colin Powell. Anyone who could defend the weapons of mass destruction program could market alcopops in their sleep. Unfortunately, just like a shiny new crate of Fat Frogs, these 'intelligent drones' have the potential to cause a lot of unnecessary carnage.

⚡ Call the Authorities ⚡

It is surprising that Irish women don't have a natural abhorrence of all things alcohol related, considering a lot of them had fathers who were heavy drinkers.

If an Irish girl was lucky, her father would fall into the category of happy drunk, staggering in the door at closing time, singing and full of the craic. Once the Drunken Dad passed out on the couch the kids would emerge from the shadows in their pyjamas and sneak down the stairs to steal all the loose change from his pockets. Shrapnel would be all that remained as their mother had usually beaten them to it and absconded with any available banknotes. In more extreme cases, the Irish Mammy would take a frying pan to her already unconscious husband and give him a couple of lashes before removing all valuables from his pockets. When he eventually regained consciousness, the alarm would be raised and the relevant authorities contacted as poor Daddy had been mugged on the way home from the pub.

Many Irish fathers worked long hours then went straight to the pub after work, and 99% of the child rearing fell to the Irish Mammy. To this day, it doesn't matter how drunken and useless an Irish woman's father is, his daughter will love him unconditionally. She gives very little credit to her long-suffering, hard-working mother, but will fawn all over her father whenever he manages to make an appearance – key evidence (as if it were needed) that alcoholism is much more socially acceptable in Ireland than martyrdom.

The father–daughter relationship is one of the most important in a girl's life. The type of men that women date and have long-term relationships with is directly related to the kind of relationship a girl has with her father. In keeping with this theory, once an Irish girl has grown up and left the family home she often turns around and marries someone who is 'fond of the drink' herself, thereby perpetuating the cycle of addiction. Nowadays, there are far more addictions and disorders to choose from, but Irish women tend to opt for the old, reliable alcoholism as it's best to stay within your comfort zone. Marrying an overeater or a sex addict sounds exhausting, and you know where you are with a drinker. You would think that an element of self-preservation would predispose them to marry workaholics, but this is not usually the case.

⋎ Cultural Norms ⋎

Finally, the following cultural norms indicate that an Irish woman's attitude to alcohol is ultimately an unhealthy one:

* In order not to drink alcohol on a night out an Irish woman has to pretend to be on antibiotics.

* When she announces that she is not drinking because she is on antibiotics, everyone will automatically assume that she is pregnant.

* The only times Irish women ever give up drink are when they are pregnant or during the month of November. To the best of this author's knowledge, there is no correlation between the two events.

* Irish women do not consider drinking wine with a meal to qualify as alcohol consumption. Wine is viewed as more of a soft drink.

* Sober flirtation is an oxymoron.

* No Irish woman has ever had a one-night stand while sober, ever, in the history of the universe.

* Blackouts are considered a minor inconvenience – on a par with getting a cold sore or maybe cystitis.

* Next to education, seven vodkas and a portion of curry chips is the most important social equaliser of our times.

Irrespective of the above, there have been some slight improvements to the nation's attitude towards alcohol in recent times. Drink-driving has greatly reduced, especially in urban areas, and nowadays it is not unheard of for an Irish woman to go the the pub, have a couple of soft drinks and drive home. Although everyone will still assume that she is with child, she can no longer expect to be treated like a social pariah because she is abstaining from drink on a night out. For the pre-iPhone generations, waking up after a heavy night's drinking used to involve crawling out of bed and calling their friends from a landline to piece together the events of the night. But now that an Irish girl's every drunken antic is recorded and posted online, we may find that public humiliation is the single deterrent that curbs our nation's propensity towards heavy drinking. Perhaps this is why today's Irish girls are breaking the mould by occasionally going on dates where they drink coffee and have sober conversations.

7.

Irish Women at Play

Irish women are not natural hobbyists. We are too busy working full-time, rearing children, compulsively cleaning our homes, checking our smartphones every four minutes, maintaining eight best friends, thirty-seven close friends and six hundred Facebook friends, and going on the piss. Very few Irish women maintain long-term hobbies, but we're prone to trying a variety of activities for a short period of time.

⚡ The GAA ⚡

Sport is something that is played by young Irish girls who were born and reared in the countryside. Although the GAA's primary focus is playing Irish sports both in Ireland and abroad, the organisation also provides a support network for Irish people throughout the world. It has helped many young Irish emigrants in obtaining jobs, accommodation and husbands. Irish women who join the GAA usually choose between playing either camogie or gaelic. These two sports can be roughly translated as hurling and gaelic for ladies. The main difference between the male and female versions is the size of the ball and the elevated level of aggression in the ladies' games. The Ladies' Gaelic Football Association or LGFA should not be confused with any lesbian or gay-friendly groups as they are two very different things.

Playing sports in Ireland often necessitates the baring of flesh and running around after a ball in the rain. All sports pitches are located in the middle of a bog. Once the summer arrives and there is a slim chance that the selected sport could be played in sunshine, the season is declared to be over until normal misery is resumed. Whinging is not tolerated, if Cúchulainn could endure sprinting around in the muck and the pouring rain then any self-respecting Mayo woman better knuckle down and get on with it. To further add to the discomfort, sporty women are expected to wear shiny nylon tops, very short shorts and knee socks.

This is not a good look for an Irish woman. It's hard to look attractive when you have knobbly knees and muck-encrusted thighs, festooned with a spattering of freckles and a savage outbreak of goosebumps. The more hirsute among us can be seen dashing around the pitch displaying legs like Chewbacca. If these girls move to the city for college or work, they join the city's camogie club for the first two months of urban life. Once the GAA has furnished them with a flat and a job, and they have pulled a garda in Coppers, they deduce that getting up early on a Sunday morning to play a match is interfering with their drinking habit and the requisite savage craic with said member of the Garda Síochána. And so, their sporting career comes to an abrupt end.

⚡ Youthful Hobbies ⚡

Many Irish girls – especially in the 1980s and 90s – were forced into taking piano lessons and Irish dancing classes; pastimes that no one ever seemed to enjoy. The piano teachers would look prim and professional, but inside there lurked extreme sado-masochistic tendencies. Underneath the piano they stashed a selection of razor-sharp bamboo sticks with which they habitually beat their students' exposed knuckles whenever they played an errone-ous note. It lent an air of menace to the aptly entitled 'Chopsticks'.

Irish dancing goes hand in hand with the dreaded *Feis Ceol*. For the uninformed, or maybe just Dubliners, a *Feis Ceol* is a combined beauty pageant and frenzied dance tournament. Irish mothers are rabidly competitive when it comes to their daughters' performance in a *Feis Ceol*, and participants are made up to look like the Bride of Chucky. Their hair is curled into an array of ringlets and a minimum of four cans of hairspray is unleashed on their curls to ensure they stay in place until the night of the child's twenty-first birthday celebration. The dancing girl is usually dressed in a heavy green tablecloth with a picture of a golden harp on the front and some multi-coloured Celtic swirls on the back. The child then assumes the starting position with their back ramrod straight and their arms pinned to their sides. Rumour has it that some mothers superglue their child's arms into position to achieve the perfect posture. The dancers gaze into the middle distance with a manic intensity, poised and ready for the necessary twirling, soaring and cavorting. The defiance of gravity is a given; the lepping can only be described as legendary.

Irish girls in the pre-digital era often followed up these activities with a fleeting interest in stamp collecting or a spell of writing to a pen pal in France or Spain. As many of the Irish correspondents lived in rural Ireland, they never actually did anything except wander aimlessly up and down country roads. Conscious that this would make for extremely tedious reading, the girls had to improvise, and so wrote long, detailed letters about imaginary shopping trips to Dublin and wonderful family picnics on the beach. Enid Blyton's writing was dark and edgy by comparison. Their pen pal would respond with an honest account of her boring life and appeared to be in awe of her Irish pen pal's exciting existence. Once the lies were initiated, they had to be maintained. It became increasingly difficult for the Irish girl to best her previous letter, resulting in the stories becoming more and more outlandish. The Irish girl would begin to resent her pen pal for forcing her into a quagmire of lies. After a couple of months, the Irish girl was compelled to send a preposterous letter to her pen pal outlining a fictitious event like the magical afternoon she spent in the company of John Travolta and Olivia Newton John, having bumped into them on the Galway to Dublin train. This would signal the demise of the correspondence, as the Irish girl would never receive a reply.

⚡ Hobbies in your Thirties ⚡

During an Irish woman's twenties the only hobbies she partakes in are drinking, puking and shifting.

These activities happen every night of the week and leave very little time for night classes. But once she hits thirty, a strange instinct compels her to sign up for one of the following: reiki, pottery or salsa dancing. Having paid her fee in full, she will attend the first class and regale all her colleagues with stories of how much she *loves* her new hobby and how they should also sign up as there are still a couple of places left on the course. She may even hint that her natural talent could necessitate her handing in her notice in order to dedicate the rest of her life to making unusually shaped butter dishes. On the first night, she makes a superhuman effort to be friendly, eager and exhilarated – of course, this is completely exhausting and impossible to maintain. Unfortunately, she misses the second week of classes due to the flu/car trouble. By the time the third class comes along, she has ruined the experience for herself by being ridiculously overkeen and painfully enthusiastic. It is a strange predicament, and the only solution is to drop out of the class immediately and never mention it again, thus proving the hypothesis that an Irish woman will never attend more than two nights of her ten-week course. If quizzed by someone as to how she is getting on with her salsa dancing, she will mutter vague assertions about developing a prolapsed disc. She then quickly changes the subject, announcing that she is now going to devote her leisure time to studying numerology and decoding the patterns of the universe.

⚡ New Age Spirituality ⚡

There was a time when Irish spirituality and superstition were confined to the banshee, fairy folk and Catholicism. Horoscopes became popular in the 70s, but were still considered to be light entertainment as opposed to personalised life predictions. During this period, the only alternative treatment available to an Irish woman was having her tea leaves read in a dilapidated caravan parked up along the seafront of one of the country's many coastal towns.

However, this all changed once the New Age travellers landed on Irish soil in the mid 90s. As the vast majority of them were English, it was like a Cromwellian comeback tour. The crusty vans arrived in droves, packed to the brim full of children, dogs and tarot cards. Then, as if by osmosis, alternative beliefs began to seep into the Irish ether. Initially, your average Irish woman would snigger at the outlandish bullshit spouted by these dreadlocked brethren, but it wasn't long before they, too, were brandishing crystals and cleansing your chakras. You couldn't swing a cat without interfering with someone's aura. It was as if the New Age spirituality had infiltrated Ireland's ground water system. Nowadays, all Irish women are alternative health practitioners and most of them double as life coaches. The crossover between archaic spirituality and modern-day practices comes in the form of angel cards: think tarot cards with a Catholic twist.

Old-fashioned cures or remedies have morphed into natural medicines and homeopathy. Irish women are no longer encouraged to rub urine into their heads to stimulate hair growth or to run around a holly bush three times to eliminate haemorrhoids. Conversely, attending a GP is almost frowned upon and scientific treatments are also being replaced by natural medicines and white witchcraft, though today's Irish witches are more likely to sell you some gothic jewellery than to cure you with their spells.

Even the more traditional Irish woman can be seen heading off to her Wednesday night yoga class. Of course, yoga is really just a series of stretches and a respite from the drudgery of everyday existence. The most challenging aspect of a yoga class is trying to keep ten Irish women from talking for one and a half hours, and dealing with the acute embarrassment following the wind-release postures. Novice New Agers have tried to cash in on the popularity of yoga in this country, and variations include hot yoga and Pilates. Pilates is a strange practice as it is effectively a class in how to stand up straight, pull in your stomach muscles and contract your anus while holding your breath. Once you have mastered this method, you are supposed to go about your daily activities while you maintain the pose. This is more difficult than it sounds; it requires immense concentration, and your facial expression defaults to an intense scrunched-up pout that verges on the cat's arsehole look. It matters not, as all eyes are focused on your amazing abs.

⋀ The Book Club Phenomenon ⋀

The last decade saw the introduction of the Book Club. Every parish in the country had at least one in operation. Very often there were factions and splits within the organisation as Jodi Picoult and Anne Enright battled for supremacy. Initially there may have been intellectual intent behind the formation of a Book Club, but it is never long before it descends into a full-scale bitch fest.

The normal Book Club night involves a group of females meeting in a neighbour's house at 8 p.m. with each woman brandishing a bottle of wine. The hostess is supposed to provide some light snacks; a couple of bowls of peanuts and some crisps would suffice. Of course, no self-respecting Irish woman would let it be said that she didn't put on a fine spread for her turn to host. Some hostesses may take the food options to another level and bake a cake that is decorated with a picture of the night's chosen book with an accurate rendering of the cover and title. Once everyone has admired the house, the furniture and the fabulous array of food, it is time to review the chosen book. As there are no professional book reviewers present, this doesn't take very long. The majority of the women will state that they either loved it or hated it and will feel no strong compulsion to elaborate. Some may embellish slightly by saying that they liked it at the beginning but then they got sick of it and completely hated it by the end.

It is now 8.10 p.m., and the book review segment is over. For the next three hours the assembled ladies discuss the price of houses for sale in the area before casting aspersions on any of the neighbours who are not in attendance. Once the hostess begins to stifle a yawn and the wine is no longer flowing freely, it is time to wrap up the evening. The monumental task of choosing the book and the hostess for the next night looms large. No one wants to do either. Being the hostess involves

Mrs Doyle type Herculean efforts in the cooking and cleaning department. Choosing the next book involves experience working for the Diplomatic Corps. If you choose something too highbrow you will be labelled an intellectual snob, will be secretly sneered at and will ultimately be responsible for boring the arse off everyone within a ten-kilometre radius. Alternatively, if you choose something a bit lighter and more chick lit friendly, you will be labelled an airhead, will be secretly sneered at and will ultimately be responsible for boring the arse off everyone within a ten-kilometre radius. To date, the books that have generated the most enthusiasm or interesting debate among Irish women are *The Slap* and *The Room*. *The Slap* is perfect because everyone gets to rant about where they stand on slapping children (an Irish woman will usually default to 'it never did *us* any harm' while simultaneously rocking back and forth in her chair and gnawing her thumbnail down to the bone). *The Room* is popular as the reader can speculate on how they would have coped with systematic rape and confinement in one room with a small child for years on end. For the great-grandmothers of today's Book Clubbers this would have been normal day-to-day living, but in modern-day Ireland that sort of thing is frowned upon. Nowadays it's all relationships and en-suite bathrooms.

⚡ The Cook Club ⚡

During the boom years, we saw the emergence of the Cook Club. This is a bit like a Book Club but far more pretentious. A hired chef comes to your house and shows the Cook Club members how to make a number of different dishes – the attendees then get to eat the delicious food. Everyone pays €50 each to the chef and sits around sipping vino, affecting an air of sophistication and making cookery related pro-nouncements such as 'OMG! How could you possibly make such a divine roux? It's soooooo delish! I have to get mine from Marks & Spencer's, of course. I'm just FAR TOO BUSY to make my own.' Preparation for the Cook Club involves having your entire kitchen upgraded to the tune of €80,000. Following the revamp, the objective of the night is the count-less opportunities for the hostess to showcase her fabulous new room. The kitchen, in turn, has been designed to best display the wide array of impressive, expensive and totally unused cooking utensils, such as a set of Japanese premium quality kitchen knives, a gigantic oversized ladle and a mini blowtorch for scorching the top of a crème brûlée. Not to mention the completely fabulous, albeit functionless, island, strategically placed so that it blocks any direct route from one side of the room to the other. Her cookware is Le Creuset and her knives and forks are nothing less than Newbridge. This woman doesn't have plates and cups: she has Dinnerware.

Finally, the wine will be equally exquisite and chosen to complement whatever the chef is preparing, regardless of the fact that most of the assembled guests would drink slops from a bucket. Once everyone has finished eating the delish food, the chef then hands out the recipes to everyone and heads off chuckling all the way to the bank.

🏃 No-Frills Hobbies 🏃

Having attained the zenith of leisure world opulence, there was nowhere else to go but downhill. We have now reached the other end of the spectrum, and the latest trends hark back to basic, no-frills hobbies. Women who previously wouldn't climb a stairs without difficulty are now posting photos of themselves dramatically crossing the finishing line at actual, real-life races. It's all 10k this and the Women's Half Marathon that. To add insult to injury, you – the non-runner – are expected to sponsor them in their new-found mania, as all the races are charity fund-raisers.

These charitable events are making the majority of Irish women look bad, especially given that the most energetic thing they've done recently is played a bit of online poker. That experience costs money too, but the recipient was Paddy Power and not the local hospice. Fear not, there is hope for us all, as the 'Couch to 5k' app has been deemed nothing short of a miracle. Of course, some of us haven't moved from the couch phase yet, but having achieved the monumental task of downloading the app onto your smartphone, it's only a matter of time.

Another startling phenomenon is the recent popularity of sewing classes. All of a sudden it is considered trendy for a group of women to meet up of an evening and sit around sewing. Is this not the type of physical toil that we tried to leave behind us in the 1800s? What was the point in becoming educated and successful career women if we were to revert to our former seamstress ways? Did we bring about this monumental social progression to facilitate the combination of working all day then bitchin' and stitchin' all evening?

This hobby is an ideal opportunity for an Irish woman to showcase her competitive nature, however. You may think the evening would involve some light-hearted chit-chat and a general air of companionship, but instead all the women have their heads down frantically trying to be the first one to finish their patchwork fronted cushion cover. The only time they raise their heads is to glance furtively at their fellow hobbyists and assess their progress. It is not unheard of for some individuals to resort to sabotage. All it takes is a well-placed knot in your neighbour's thread or some unnecessary extra pressure applied to their sewing machine's pedal. At the end of the night everyone hobbles home, crippled, after spending four hours bent over a sewing machine, partially blinded from threading needles but triumphantly brandishing their misshapen doily.

🗡 Fight Club 🗡

In keeping with the theme of no-frills hobbies, and as a natural progression from the Book and Cook Clubs, surely it is only a matter of time before all Irish women start attending a Fight Club. Preparation for this bitch fest should not be overly expensive – the provisioning of food is unnecessary as plummeting blood sugar levels will ensure that the attendees are already on the offensive. A couple of bottles of liquor are all that is needed to raise the levels of aggression to a suitable plateau. Similarly, adapting the house for the event shouldn't be too cumbersome, although storing away any valuable, breakable items is advised. Some women will no doubt extend their houses to include a cage-fighting arena (see previous section on Cook Club kitchen extensions), thereby besting their neighbours. Also, as most Irish women are well within their comfort zone in a screaming argument, this new hobby will be ultra-inclusive.

Themes for discussion can be identified in advance. The first rule of Fight Club is that all chosen subjects must generate discord among the assembled Irish ladies, for example:

*   Round 1: The night could kick off with tax fraud and the relevance of the Irish language.

*   Round 2: The hostess should introduce the following topics:

    *   communal ex-boyfriends;

    *   soap opera spoilers; and

    *   tagging and posting unflattering photos of your friends on Facebook.

*   Round 3: Following eight vodka and whites, the ladies present will be narrowing their eyes to slits and using staccato speech to emphasise their point.

* Round 4: The *pièce de résistance* might be an in-depth analysis of the different child discipline techniques favoured by the assembled mob, followed by a comparison of how well behaved their children are.

* Round 5: If there hasn't been any skin and hair flying by this point, the hostess will be reduced to cheap and nasty tactics. A classic 'she said that you said…' shit-stirring muttered out of the side of her mouth should do the trick.

* Round 6: The culmination of the night's work could involve a plant. The hostess needs to identify someone who is prepared to yell 'Garth Brooks is a greedy shite' into the fray, then turn on her heels and scatter, with the inevitable assortment of frenzied Irish women tearing after her, hair wild, eyes rolling, stripped to the waist and frothing at the mouth.

The Fight Club would be a monumental success as, discounting any injuries sustained, all club members could engage in some one-upmanship of the 'Well, I showed her' variety; a much-loved pastime for all Irish women irrespective of their age or social standing.

So, what will be next for the active Irish woman: Handwashing Your Curtains classes or maybe Fowl Slaughtering Clubs? And let's not forget Zumba, whatever the fuck that is.

⋏ Social Media ⋌

Hobbies are not something that today's young Irish girls bother with. They are far too engrossed with the various forms of social media. In this age of globalisation, their entire justification for existence is focused on their pocket-sized social networking device – it symbolises their popularity and therefore their self-worth. In fact, nomophobia, or the fear of being without your mobile device, is now recognised as a serious affliction. However, there are still some Irish women who have no idea what a social networking application is. These ladies have obviously been living on another planet for the past ten years, or maybe just in the midlands. In order to save you time on downloading one such app and learning how to use it, and in order to minimise the risk of some horrific social networking faux pas, here is a useful guide for the Luddites among us:

* **Snapchat:** Are you the type of narcissist who loves to take pictures of yourself getting ready

for the party, going to the party, having fun at the party, leaving at the end of the party, and waking up the morning after the party? Do you feel the strange compulsion to inform the ether when you are bored/happy/sad/hungover like a dog through the medium of exaggerated facial expressions and photography? Are you then desirous of sharing those pictures with the wider world, confident in the knowledge that somebody, somewhere actually gives a shit? Perhaps you are preoccupied with flashing your bits for the more subversive Kodak moment. If you disapprove of the inherent popularity contest involved in the number of Likes, Retweets and virtual friends that people have on other applications, then Snapchat is the social networking app for you. It is the bare, stripped-back version of your online self. It is the only place where you feel liberated enough to share those horrific photos where you have five distinct chins or no visible chin whatsoever. The Snapchat enthusiast is capable of laughing heartily at themselves, but only for about three seconds and only on condition that the Dorian *Who Ate all the Pies* Gray type reproduction disappears forever and no evidence of it ever emerges at a later date. Also, the absence of any lengthy texting capabilities means that any profound messages must be communicated in a series of incomprehensible Marcel Marceau tableaux, which require far too much effort to decipher, especially given that the average Snapchat user has the attention span of a flea with ADHD. However, Snapchat does let users add personal drawings or notes to the photos and videos they send, which mostly default to the ubiquitous, life-affirming LOL.

* **Instagram:** Instagram is the glossy version of Snapchat, and is all about the filters. If Snapchat is the stripped-back version of your online self then, thanks to Instagram's ability to change the lighting or colour on an image, it offers up the Hollywood celebrity version of your average Irish gal. So reliant are they on these tweaks and edits that in a couple of decades we will have the phenomenon of the deathbed selfie, where a generation of Irish women's final requests will be for the inclusion of a flattering filter to their last ever selfie. #YOLO

* **Twitter:** The only reason Irish women use Twitter is to stalk celebrities. Any famous person with a Twitter account can be tracked down and followed by their Irish female fan base. When an Irish woman joins Twitter, the first thing she

does is search for famous people to see if they are also on Twitter, thereby identifying that she has something in common with them already. Once she has located her favourite musician, celebrity chef, politician, TV or radio personality, comedian or brand of yoghurt, she simply clicks on Follow and waits for her muse to tweet. When her hero or heroine posts a tweet, the Irish woman (read: stalker) immediately responds with 140 characters that are clever, amusing, fawning, supportive, or a combination of all four. The objective of the exercise is to have their tweet favourited or responded to by the celebrity. This will mean that for one split second the Irish gal was noticed by a famous person before they went back to counting their truckloads of money and snorting cocaine off a catwalk model's butt cheeks. When the Irish woman's other half enquires as to what the hell she is doing on that fucking phone all the time, she will casually explain that she is in the middle of a good old natter with Jay-Z. The Irish female Twitterer firmly believes that on her next world tour Kerry Perry will make a detour to Clonmel due to the special bond they have established on Twitter and the fact that she once liked a tweet posted by her favourite Irish Katycat.

* **Facebook:** Facebook is the social networking app for the 30+ generation of Irish women. Facebook allows them to share photos, videos, pictures and a large amount of text in order to keep their friends updated about what they had for dinner, what time they brought their dog for a walk (including actual video footage of the dog walking), where they went on holidays and where they stand on same-sex marriage (very firmly in favour, as it happens). Some of this information is riveting and some of it a tad mundane, but the ruination of Facebook is the horrific influx of memes (memes are those images that contain short, patronising catchphrases designed to give a life-affirming message to the reader). They began their life as emails that, once shared with all your friends, would guarantee long life or the immediate arrival of wealth or happiness. They have since morphed into a rampant motivational speech virus that has infected the Facebook application. A sort of mass sound bite of 'wake up and smell the roses' messages designed to make you appreciate what you have, treat everyone with respect and live your life to the full, e.g. hand in your notice and pursue that lifelong dream of home-made jam production. The use of memes allows an Irish woman to quote the Dalai Lama to her friends, and by proxy to appear wise and spiritual and bursting with inner peace and happiness. Most people try to scroll past them on their newsfeed, but they draw you in, like the digital equivalent of rubbernecking at a road traffic accident. Rather than inspiring the reader they make you feel shallow, insipid and uninspired. In essence, the Facebook meme has replaced the Catholic Church as the number one provider of feelings of inadequacy in an Irish woman's life. The under-30s are scornful of wisdom and have very little interest in sage advice, so it is not surprising that they have no time for Facebook and it is now considered to be extremely uncool among the younger generation of Irish females. They're all still on it, but they only ever log in to use its stalking functionality, which cannot be bested by any other app. To them, Facebook is like a really shit party full of losers and old people that they cannot leave for the simple reason that everyone is there.

8.

The Fabulous Irish Mammy

Discipline and School Gate Etiquette

Proud, ashamed, love them, hate them, equal parts rabidly competitive and sneeringly dismissive; this is how an Irish woman feels towards her children. The obsessive adoration that an Irish Mammy feels towards her children is manic, psychotic and verging on downright creepy. Some newbie mothers claim to love their firstborns so much that they have to make a conscious efforts not to actually eat them. But once that first baby is born, the Irish woman will never again have the luxury of being able to read a paper, finish a sentence or eat a hot meal – and they don't actually care, because nothing overshadows their primary role of being an Irish Mammy. They no longer have their own identity and will live the rest of their lives vicariously through their children. Even the most cut-throat businesswoman turns to putty when she sees a photo of a baby in a bucket with a headpiece fashioned like an oversized daisy. No one will ever love you as much as your Irish Mammy does. It doesn't matter how embarrassing you find this – it's not going to go away. An Irish Mammy's love is not something that will eventually wear off, and no amount of emigration to Australia, murdering someone or marrying a foreigner will put her off or diffuse that love.

⋏ Proportional Representation of an ⋏ Irish Mother's Love

If you were lucky enough to be born the son of an Irish Mammy you will obviously get far more love and affection than your sisters. The below chart gives a rough guide to the division of an Irish mother's love:

* **Son who is a qualified doctor:** Congratulations! You are the primary beneficiary of your mother's love. Nothing you say or do will dislodge you from this position. There may have been times earlier

Percentage of an Irish Mother's Love

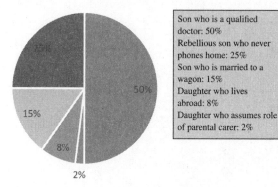

Son who is a qualified doctor: 50%
Rebellious son who never phones home: 25%
Son who is married to a wagon: 15%
Daughter who lives abroad: 8%
Daughter who assumes role of parental carer: 2%

in your life when you found this adoration a bit cringeworthy, but as the years went by you managed to get over it. In hindsight, having to endure a couple of years of public maternal preening and fussing was a small price to pay for seven years of college fees and free childcare for your own offspring when the need arose.

* **Rebellious son who never phones home:** If you are the black sheep of the family who rarely contacts your mother unless you're in need of a financial bailout, you, too, will receive a high proportion of your mother's love. In fact, your mother will devote her entire life to defending your behaviour and proving that you have

turned over a new leaf and have changed your selfish ways.

* **Son who is married to a wagon:** They say that all Irish men marry women who are just like their mothers. If you do marry a woman who has similar personality traits to your own mother, it will not end well. Your new wife may misguidedly believe that she is now the most important woman in your life. She may become a competitor in the fabulous Mammy competition and feel obliged to indicate to your mother that she has transformed you into a healthy-eating, smart-dressing Adonis. During a maternal visit your spouse may even shrilly request that your mother desists from dusting the tops of your wardrobes and refrains from running her finger along the tops of your skirting boards. Throw a couple of bottles of Sangre de Toro into the mix and there will be tears shed and doors banged by bedtime. You will be caught in the crossfire and this is a very uncomfortable place to be. Sitting on the fence is not an option; you are forced into choosing between a reduction in maternal love and a reduction in conjugal rights. We all know what the outcome of that particular Sophie's Choice will be, and the end result is being relegated to a meagre 15% of your Irish Mammy's love.

* **Daughter who lives abroad:** Although you will never attain the same levels of love and affection as your brothers do due to the fact that you are living abroad, you will receive the most mother–daughter love. Your Mammy delights in being worried sick about you, constantly fretting about you contracting Ebola or being captured and sold to sex traffickers. Ultimately, your Irish Mammy is thrilled to have an excuse for all this maternal concern, despite your assurances that your new day-to-day existence in Sheffield is relatively humdrum and uneventful.

* **Daughter who assumed role of parental carer:** The day comes when the Irish Mammy grows weak and feeble and needs daily care and domestic support. The role of maternal carer always falls to one of her daughters. It is inevitable that the daughter who lives closest to the old family home will assume this role. One would expect that the provision of this service guarantees exalted levels of love and affection, but this is rarely the case. The Irish Mammy will detest being dependent on you and resent your intrusion. Your standards of cleaning will be inferior, and any attempt you make to organise your mother's schedule will be perceived as elderly bullying. Simultaneously, you,

the carer, will grow bitter and twisted and will no longer be able to clasp eyes on your own mother without hissing at her like a venomous witch. Being Irish, neither party will ever discuss their feelings or explain their behaviour and so the cycle of familial resentment spins on, the inevitable conclusion being the death of the old Irish Mammy and the subsequent adoption of all her character defects by her daughter.

⚡ Parenting Styles ⚡

In the 60s, when a baby was born no emphasis was placed on bonding, eating the placenta or skin-on-skin contact. *Au contraire*, many Irish Mammies smoked in the maternity ward and most of them had a locker full of booze so they could offer their visitors a drink. It was more like visiting a hygienic brothel full of tired and overworked hookers than a maternity ward. These mothers never suffered from the guilt that today's working mothers feel. Resentment was more the order of the day, as many of them had given up jobs and cut their hair short when they fell pregnant. There was no longer any reason for them to look attractive as breeding was complete, and similarly their working life was considered to be finito. A guilty mother is more inclined to spoil her kids and pander to their every whim, whereas a resentful mother is like a walking time bomb, going through the domestic motions whilst seething internally at their early retirement from life.

Parenting styles and discipline techniques have changed drastically in just one lifetime. The previous generation of Irish Mammies could never be accused of over-parenting: they were quite comfortable leaving their kids in the car for hours on end with two and a half crayons to keep them amused. There was no 'time out' or 'naughty step' back in the good old days; instead there was proper physical punishment in the form of a skelp to the back of the knees with the dreaded wooden spoon. Even the mere threat of the wooden spoon was enough to put the fear of God into any Irish child. Many mothers had a drawer in the kitchen devoted solely to these domiciliary batons, which they would rattle in a menacing fashion whenever their children were acting up – much in the same way that movie gangsters push their jacket to one side to reveal their holstered gun. The message is simple: I have a concealed weapon and I'm not afraid to use it. The very act of opening the wooden spoon drawer was enough to quell any rebellion.

⚡ The Fabulous Mammy ⚡ Competition

When it comes to their children, Irish women are infinitely competitive (see Chapters 5 & 7). From the first time an Irish woman parades her new baby in a buggy, she will secretly peer into the other buggies passing by and grade them on their appearance. She will exhale a sigh of relief as, luckily, none of the other minger babies can compare to her little bundle of cuteness.

No matter how ugly or mediocre an Irish woman's child is, they will firmly believe that their child is a talented prodigy with movie star looks. If the child gets crap results in school, blame will be assigned to their friends, the useless teacher or the lack of Feng Shui in the classroom. The Irish Mammy cannot cope with the possibility that her child might just be a bit dim. If the child's team loses a match, it will be blamed on their coach or the fact that the opposing team were twice their age sporting fully grown beards.

Football pitches all over the country are lined with frenzied Irish Mammies. They jump up and down, screaming and swearing until their voices go hoarse. It is not unheard of for an Irish Mammy to rush onto the pitch cursing at and accosting one of the players, usually her own child: 'What the fuck are you doing?', 'Keep your eye on the ball' and 'Take the bastard down!' are some of the words of parental encouragement proffered by Irish Mammies during your typical under-eights friendly match. The minute the whistle blows and the mania dissipates, all retreating mothers can be heard agreeing that it's all just a bit of fun and that winning is immaterial as it's the participation that counts.

Irish women insist on boring everyone to death with cutesy stories of what their kids said and did. This is also a thinly veiled competition. If one mother's child called someone an 'asshole' (usually Granny) at the age of three, another mother will immediately counter-attack with the heart-warming account of her two-year-old telling someone to 'fuck off'. Not to be bested, there will always be someone in the group who will insist that her child's first word was 'cuntyhooks'.

⚔ (Aside) The 3rd C-word ⚔

This brings us to the third C-word with which Irish women have an uncomfortable relationship: 'cunt'. 99% of Irish women refuse to utter the word, will tut if they hear anyone else using it and quickly assert that they hate the word with a passion. However, these selfsame ladies have no problem lashing the word 'fuck' into every sentence. The reluctance to utter the former has resulted in the 'See You Next Tuesday' acronym, as in 'he was a right C U Next Tuesday'. The remaining 1% of the Irish female population find this dilution insulting to the swear word. A person either uses the swear word or they don't, and any kind of cutesy phrasing is a cop out. When in polite society, however, an Irish woman may pause, hors d'oeuvres in hand, to proclaim: 'It's not a word I would normally use, but yer man is only a cunt.' (End of aside)

Many Irish women feel the need to entertain their friends with a detailed account of what their child does or doesn't eat. They would have us believe that their child hates junk food and loves to eat salad and scallops. These are the type of mothers who announce in a restaurant at the top of their voices that their toddler wouldn't dream of eating anything from the children's menu. The inference is that only a top-class, first-grade mother would have a child who hates pizza and chicken nuggets. Although the rivalry may appear to be about the children, it is really a Fabulous Mammy Tournament, and only the truly devoted need apply. Mothers who bake, meet a minimum of four out of the five a day dietary requirements, regularly initiate fun craft days (oxymoron), spend four evenings a week ferrying their children to meet their ever-changing hobby needs and volunteer for every parental event in their children's school would be typical contestants. Mothers whose kids have head lice would not.

⋏ Criticising an Irish Mammy's ⋏ Children

No matter how much an Irish woman gives out about her child, you must never agree with her. This is a trap, and you must tread carefully. No one is allowed to criticise an Irish Mammy's child except the Mammy herself; if you so much as murmur vague assent she will turn on you like a rabid she-wolf. No matter what behaviour her child indulges in, an Irish Mammy will always defend it. When they are toddlers and have an off-the-charts temper tantrum in the middle of a supermarket or systematically demolish a neighbour's house, their mother will excuse it by stating that they are 'overtired'. As they get a little older and become precocious little brats who have never benefitted from a minute's discipline, they are said to be 'spirited'. Failing that, a sudden diagnosis of ADHD will appear as if by magic.

Time goes by and children turn into teenagers; psychotic tendencies that were previously only hinted at will mature and flourish. There is no excusing or defending a teenager's antisocial ways, but the Irish Mammy's resilience is legendary and she will come up with a detailed account of their altruistic endeavours. If they have never actually done anything nice for anyone, she will resort to pronouncements about how much her surly fourteen-year-old adores babies, puppies and lambs.

⚡ School Gate Etiquette ⚡

If you rarely spend any time at the school gates, you will be unversed in the protocol and unused to the typical characters in attendance. The following guidelines on the types of parents you will encounter there may prove beneficial.

Yummy Mummy

This mother has a full face of make-up and has freshly washed and straightened hair. She is usually dressed in a dark coloured, co-ordinated outfit and drives a black people-carrier or four-by-four, aka the Terenure Tank. She moves fast; whether it's her driving style or the way she dashes into the schoolyard to retrieve her child, she generates the semblance of busyness. Be under no illusion; she will never be your friend as she is FAR TOO BUSY and has way more important things to do than make idle chit-chat at the school gates. People are often intimidated by Yummy Mummy and presume that she is judging them ... and they are probably right. Rest assured, her days are numbered and she is living on borrowed time. Both the Bank and NAMA will soon come a knockin' on the door of her primary home. Note: this is the Irish mother most likely to be addicted to prescription pills.

Earth Mother

In the past, this mother was typically non-Irish. The Earth Mother was traditionally English or from northern Europe, but nowadays more and more Irish Mammies are adopting the Earth Mother persona. She usually wears colourful mismatched floral or beaded clothing and crocs or flip-flops. She is extremely friendly and knows all the names of the other mothers, the teachers and 90% of the kids. In fact, the Earth Mother probably knows more about your children than you do. This type of mother is so dedicated to her children, and by proxy her children's school, that she volunteers for all the school events. Most Saturdays she can be spotted at the end of your checkout in Dunnes Stores bagging people's shopping to raise money for the school library. This practice is utterly humiliating both for the bagger and the bagee. You would retain more dignity dressing as a medieval peasant and being put in stocks for the weekend. Ludicrous as this suggestion sounds, Earth Mother would be the first woman with her hand up volunteering for this 'fun-filled and worthwhile' event.

GAA Mam

The GAA Mam is usually easy to spot as she will be wearing tight high-waist denims or a tracksuit and runners. Her hair will be in a ponytail and she will have healthy ruddy cheeks and no make-up. The only time she changes her look is on Sundays when she gets dressed up for Mass. She is usually the loudest of the mothers, and it is not unheard of for GAA Mam to be heard swearing profusely while waiting at the school gates. As the cursing is related to the results of last weekend's Gaelic football match, all school authorities will turn a blind eye.

Recently Laid-Off Dad

He is the guy with his eyes downcast, shuffling his feet and looking extremely uncomfortable. There is no point in trying to engage him in conversation as he is pretending that he is not actually present. At best, he will answer any direct questions with a grunt. He is not warming to his new role of stay-at-home dad, and begrudges having to help with homework and make sandwiches. To add to his resentment, he firmly believes that his wife is spending all day in the office flirting with her colleagues, filing her nails and faffing around on the internet while he is being forced to mingle with a gaggle of dangerously over-friendly women. The closest he has previously come to this many enthusiastic females was when he was on a stag night and they hooked up with a hen party. On that occasion, the combination of alcohol and dildo-shaped accessories helped to alleviate the tension between the sexes.

Modern Dad

Modern Dad is the antithesis of Recently Laid-Off Dad. He is brimming with friendliness and nauseating enthusiasm. He is so in touch with his feminine side that he is not ashamed to admit to baking with the kids and watching daytime television. Modern Dad is perfectly comfortable with his role in life. However, it is not unheard of for Modern Dad to manipulate you into taking all his children on a play date, thereby freeing himself to indulge in his favourite pastime, that of doing fuck all. He is so at ease in himself that he doesn't mind causing the following reactions:

* Recently Laid-Off Dad glowers at him with genuine hatred and vows that he will take a job in McDonald's for fear of metamorphosing into Modern Dad.

* GAA Mam is somewhat confused. She presumes that Modern Dad is gay, yet he has a wife and children. Whatever the explanation, she is not comfortable in his presence and will stare unblinkingly ahead if he attempts to engage her in conversation.

* It is unlikely that Yummy Mummy will notice him. If she does, she will treat him with the same lofty friendliness she reserves for her cleaner.

The relationship between Earth Mother and Modern Dad is a complex one. In essence, they are competing with one another for the title of most delightful and devoted parent. Although they greet one another with smiles and hugs, under the surface they are a seething mass of antagonism.

⋀ An Irish Mammy's Worst Nightmare ⋀

An Irish Mammy's worst fear – more than head lice, starvation or death – is being found out by the neighbours. It doesn't matter if they are not actually engaged in any nefarious activities, they live in perpetual fear of being rumbled. This causes them a lot of unnecessary worries. Some classic examples include: what if one of their offspring got knocked down and, upon arrival in A & E, was found to have skid marks on their underpants? A teenage son or daughter falls in the door at 2 a.m. covered in blood and vomit and the first concern for the Irish Mammy is not 'What happened?' or 'Are you all right?' but 'Did anyone see you?'

What if Obama were secretly visiting Ireland, whereupon he got lost, arrived at an Irish Mammy's door and she had no ham sandwiches or alcohol in the house? Would she really care if Barack left the house hungry and sober? The real concern for an Irish Mammy is not the event in itself but the thought of the neighbours finding out. This worry has caused many Irish women to drive themselves into an early grave, handwashing curtains and perpetually cleaning grout with a toothbrush. Above all, the neighbours must never know about any money troubles, alcoholism, depression or unsightly domestic staining. Every now and again there will be an event like the Stations of the Cross or a Book Club night that necessitates all the neighbours penetrating an Irish woman's fortress. In essence, it is a spot check by an Irish Mammy's peers. Once inside, all the other Irish Mammies will take the opportunity to scrutinise your home carefully for any fault lines or indications of internal distress. There is a comparative phenomenon in the natural world where locusts, which are normally quite solitary insects, have a behavioural period called the gregarious phase. When environmental conditions yield many green plants, locusts congregate into thick, mobile, ravenous swarms. Similarly, an Irish wake or a Holy Communion invokes hordes of Irish females who descend on your home, lay waste to your ham sandwiches and infest your house in a seething mass of intrusiveness.

Do you sometimes feel like you were drugged with chloroform, plucked from your previous windswept and interesting existence and deposited into a life of domesticity and motherhood? Perhaps your present day-to-day life is really part of some top-secret witness protection program? Do you have any recollection of actually agreeing to saddle yourself with never-ending debt, monogamy and parental responsibility? If you answered yes to any of these questions, you will likely need some help in preparing your home for any upcoming Peer Reviews.

An Irish Mammy should prepare for this onslaught by arranging their household items as follows:

Kitchen area

Display: home-baked goods on a metal rack (can be purchased in advance and removed from plastic packaging), some new hipster food like kale or linseed flax (which would be better put to use in fabric production than food preparation), a selection of celebrity cookbooks and some of your children's artwork (your offspring's masterpieces can usually be located at the bottom of their schoolbags. If you cannot find any, simply draw something a bit shite yourself and display on your fridge using an amusing fridge magnet).

Hide: all empty bottles that once contained alcohol, all overdue bills and any food that has been in the fridge so long that it has grown flagella and become self-propelling.

Medicine cabinet

Display: a range of homeopathic treatments, overpriced hair products and anything made from seaweed.

Hide: head lice treatment, Preparation H, pregnancy tests, used cotton buds, sleeping tablets and all forms of anti-depressants.

Bedroom

Display: a couple of Orla Kiely cushions casually strewn on top of the bed, a carefully selected pile of books on the bedside locker that range from *Fifty Shades of Grey* to *The Artist's Way*, an accompanying notebook and pen for recording creative thoughts that flash unbidden into your brain at 6.30 a.m., some silk nightwear and some scented oils.

Hide: dirty socks and knickers, dirty plates and cups, *Bella* and *Hello!* magazines, jars of Vaseline and any cheap and nasty sex toys.

Once the house has been thus prepped, you are ready for your Peer Review.

⚡ Control Freaks ⚡

By virtue of neighbourly pressure and parental pride, all Irish Mammies are becoming control freaks. It would be impossible to maintain these clean room standards without being manically obsessive. This preoccupation with hygiene has produced a new phenomenon, and there has been a noticeable trend towards Obsessive Compulsive Disorder among many Irish Mammies. The disorder is mostly linked to standards of hygiene. Irish Mammies are increasingly prone to carrying around Marigold gloves in their handbags for when they have to use a public bathroom. If Marigolds aren't an option, they're reduced to stretching their jumper down over their hands to flush a public toilet. Indeed, many Irish women refuse to do a poo anywhere but in the comfort of their own homes. These Stepford Wives type standards bring with them some incumbent health risks. A two-week holiday in Lanzarote can result in septicaemia. Irish women should never visit India as the mental strain of witnessing casual public defecation on the streets of Mumbai will drive them over the edge. Unable to cope with this horror, their minds shut down and they will undoubtedly return home wearing Arabian Nights style baggy trousers and bindis and babbling Paolo Coelho quotes; a condition from which many never recover.

Having OCD has almost become trendy, and in keeping with her competitive nature an Irish woman will attempt to appear more OCD than her peers. An Irish Mammy's OCD can range from repeatedly getting out of bed in the middle of the night to make sure all external windows and doors are locked to the practice of extreme hoarding. Due to ridiculously high standards of cleanliness and the need to be the most fabulous Mammy in the world ever, they are unrivalled in the anxiety disorder stakes. Ask any Irish woman today if she suffers from OCD and she will gaily recount all her mental ticks and psychological glitches:

* How she has to stand in the middle of her kitchen floor then leap from tile to tile to leave the room, thus ensuring that she never steps on any lines.

* How she hoovers the curtains, pours gallons of peroxide down her toilets, repeatedly irons her socks and blesses herself six times after the Angelus.

* How she leaves the house every day then immediately doubles back to check that the oven/iron/hair straightener is switched off.

* How she drives herself crazy by repeatedly uttering the word 'Bye' when she is hanging up the phone.

Most of these women are unsure what the OCD acronym stands for, but they know they have it in spades. Better still, they have it worse than anyone else. Some years ago there was a memorable ad for household hygiene that served to exacerbate these symptoms.

The ad was filmed as if the viewer were wearing night-vision goggles and following the Irish Mammy as she went about her daily chores. She began by chopping up a raw chicken breast on the countertop and the next scenes showed the germs that were bursting forth from the chicken as glowing radioactive organisms. Scare tactics included the subsequent spreading of these germs by the slovenly Irish Mammy as she rubbed them in her hair, over the countertops, transferred them to her children's backs and patted them all over the dog. Nobody was safe from this diseased Irish woman and her contaminated fingers. While the ad invoked consternation among the female population of Ireland, they think nothing of pissing in public and vomiting into their handbag on a night out, but shudder in revulsion at the sight of some uncooked poultry.

9.

An Irish Woman Abroad

A Profound Insight into the Erratic Behaviour of Irish Women on Holidays

If the Earth were formed at midnight, and the present moment is the following midnight, some twenty-four hours later, then Irish women have only been going on sun holidays since 11.59.59 p.m., i.e. for approximately one second. This analogy highlights the fact that for the majority of Irish women a vacation is a relatively new phenomenon. Irish women didn't start having holidays of any type until the 70s, and initially the practice involved packing hordes of screaming children into a Morris Minor and driving to a different county to visit Granny. During the 80s the Irish holiday progressed to the rental of holiday cottages in seaside towns like Bundoran or Salthill. Then came the days of walking into a travel agency, handing over your travel dates and being given the option of Cyprus, the Greek islands or Fuengirola as your holiday destination. You had a quick look at some resort brochures with photos of spacious apartments and tanned holidaymakers, beaming with happiness. You then chose one of the three resorts and handed over a cheque for the full amount, blissfully unaware that you would never stay in such a flat or be such a person.

⚡ Holiday Cottages ⚡

But before the dawn of the sun holiday, Irish families would take one holiday a year if they were lucky and would drive to a rented holiday home for two weeks with a selection of aunties and cousins. The holiday cottage visits bore an uncanny resemblance to today's survivalist shows. The living conditions were primitive, food was scarce or inedible and, in keeping with the *I'm a Celebrity...* formula, there was widespread terror invoked by infestations of creepy crawlies. By the end of the family vacation no one would be on speaking terms. Most children of the 80s will remember these holidays as times when you would sit inside a freezing cold house, looking out of the window at the rain bucketing down. The mindless boredom would prompt trips to the beach, where the children would be encouraged to engage in the futile practice of building sandcastles out of sodden wet sand.

It was usually better for the younger generation if the rain didn't stop, because if there was even a brief pause in the downpour you would be forced into the sea for a swim. No amount of tears or faked asthma attacks would get you off the hook as you were on your HOLIDAYS and therefore expected to race into the Arctic-like waters and play around with unbridled enthusiasm. Almost immediately, your feet would go numb and turn an alarming shade of magnolia with a purplish tinge. It was as if you had already died of exposure and rigor mortis was kicking in. The intense cold caused breathing difficulties, and the only way to prevent cardiac arrest was to jump up and down and run around in the water screaming. Any adults in attendance would be safely positioned on the shore or sometimes huddled in the car wearing woolly jumpers and raincoats. There was much self-congratulation when they saw their offspring cavorting around in the grey, choppy waters of the Atlantic having a fabulous time. Proof, as if it were needed, that the holiday was a resounding success.

Once the torturous swim was over, you were encouraged to go fishing with some newly purchased fishing nets. Within the first ten minutes the bamboo handle and the green net would have parted ways and you were reduced to holding the net in your hand and crouching over a rock pool, repeatedly scooping out small stones and bits of seaweed. Once you had tormented the resident crab for a period of time and hacked a resistant mollusc off a rock, the fishing portion of the day would have exhausted its entertainment potential. As a last resort you would wander up and down the beach collecting shells and the dismembered limbs of some foolhardy crabs and placing them in a plastic bucket. Each child would insist on bringing their seaside booty back to the holiday home and dumping the smelly contents of the bucket onto a sideboard where the humming mass would remain for the rest of the holiday.

The holiday homes were almost always dismal places. On arrival there would be a certain amount of concern at the lack of central heating throughout the house. Still, at least there was usually a quaint open fireplace. Every evening all the family members would gather in the sitting room in anticipation of a roaring fire and some spontaneous *sean nós* storytelling. However, it was impossible to stay in the room for longer than five minutes as the chimney would persistently billow out clouds of smoke. All household members would end up doubled over in coughing spasms from smoke inhalation with tears streaming down their faces and would be forced to crawl out of the room for fear of death by asphyxiation. It was usually safest to retreat to the bedroom and creep under the covers in an attempt to get warm, but, unsurprisingly, the bedclothes would be mouldy and damp having lain there undisturbed since the previous September. There are abnormally high instances of childhood asthma in this country, which can be traced back to holidaying in quaint rural cottages and enforced paddling in sub-zero temperatures.

Toilets were often located in a shed at the back of the house, and cooking facilities consisted of a double gas ring and a tiny oven. And if the accoutrements were poor, the cooking ingredients were even worse. Provisions would be purchased from the local shop, as this would typically be the only retail outlet within a thirty-mile radius. Inside there was always a plethora of overpriced, out-of-date, boxed food. As a result, evening meals would consist of burgers that instantly shrivelled up once they were exposed to heat, like a spider in an electric bar heater, and with comparable nutritional value. These were served with a mountain of Smash (i.e. radioactive mashed potatoes in a box) and some tinned spaghetti hoops. The bread was always stale and the boxes of Galtee cheese had so many additives in them that they glowed in the dark. This was handy if you needed to use the toilet after nightfall and couldn't locate the torch. Dessert consisted of tinned pears, dayglo instant Bird's Angel Delight or sweaty Swiss rolls with powdered custard. The pudding pleasures were second to none. It was as if the local shopkeeper were expecting a nuclear holocaust and knew the futility of stocking fresh produce.

⋏ Bushtucker Trial ⋏

There was usually an infestation of spiders or earwigs in the rental home, and the turf basket was their Trojan horse. They would attach themselves to the underside of the turf outside and lay low until it was thrown into the turf basket, carried indoors and placed beside the fire. Once inside, they would come streaming out and lay siege to the house's inhabitants. These creepy crawlies would be teeming around in your hair, your pockets and inside your pillowcase. Even the simple act of spinning the toilet roll would result in four or five insects being launched from between the sheets and onto your exposed lap.

There were often other, more serious, insect incidents. Young children getting attacked by wasps (the correct local pronunciation being asp, like the snake, with a w- in front of it) was a common occurrence. This typically happened during one of the holiday's endless and pointless meanders up and down the nearby country roads. The wasp would attach itself onto someone's neck, causing them to stumble around screaming with their arms flailing wildly, like an extra from *Aliens*. Eventually, the toxic stinger would fall off the hysterical child's neck and they would be bundled off to the local pub for a therapeutic mineral and a soothing bag of Tayto. These particular vacations were reminiscent of one long, drawn-out Bushtucker Trial.

⚡ Fáilte Ireland ⚡

Integrating with the locals was always part of the holiday fun. Their Fáilte Ireland tactics usually consisted of scaring the shit out of the blow-ins. During an encounter with a local farmer or shopkeeper, the holidaying children would be regaled with stories about tragic local accidents or the recent sightings of the banshee in the area. When Ireland does fairies, they never look like Cate Blanchett or Liv Tyler. The Irish banshee is a mythological old hag with stringy grey hair, rotten teeth and fiery red eyes. The storyteller would indicate a spot nearby where the fiendish fairy had been seen and embellish the tale with their rendition of the banshee's wail.

Following these heart-warming storytelling sessions, the walk back to the holiday cottage became a terrifying experience for the young Irish tourists. Dusk would have fallen and, collectively, they would pick up the pace to an anxious jog. Finally, one child would crack and start to run at full speed. The kids would be driven by mass hysteria into a manic sprint. No one wanted to bring up the rear and therefore find themselves within reach of the evil hag's clutches. Just as their Irish Mammies were starting to worry about them, the door of the cottage would burst open and they would fall in through the door, sobbing hysterically in a half-crazed condition. That was always the highlight of the kids' summer holidays.

⋏ Holidays Abroad ⋏

We have moved on from the 80s' holiday 'glamour' and nowadays it's all Fuerteventura this and Lanzarote that, although 'staycations' have experienced a come-back in the very recent past. When queuing in an airport for a flight check-in, it's usually easy to spot the Irish women who are travelling abroad. They will have collapsed in a heap onto their mountain of luggage and will look more like refugees fleeing their war-torn homeland than happy holidaymakers embarking on a two-week sun holiday. The simple act of booking and packing for the holiday has nearly resulted in a mental breakdown and the majority of Irish women would be better off checking into the nearest psychiatric unit than spending two weeks in a Turkish resort.

Preparation for the holiday commenced some ten months earlier and has been an endless round of online research of villas, hotels, apartments, standards of beaches, prices of flights, car rental deals, restaurants in the area and potential day trips. The arrival of online holiday booking has truly been ruinous for Irish women. The simple act of booking a holiday has become a gargantuan task; they have far too many options and cannot commit to making a decision. An Irish woman's work output will have suffered drastically in the ten month lead-in as the holiday research will consume at least four hours of an eight-hour workday, with two hours being spent viewing sun-kissed holidaymakers stretched out on sumptuous sun loungers in exotic locations, and the other two hours reading endless boring reviews on TripAdvisor. It's twenty hours a week of online holiday porn.

The Google Maps satellite setting has become a game changer. You can now see exactly how far it really is to walk to the beach, you have full visibility of the building site located right next door to your holiday home and can window-shop at the local *supermercado*.

This is the online version of curtain twitching, and all in the name of research – a perfect pastime for an Irish woman. If you want to stretch the researcher/stalker role to its absolute limit, you can stake out the front door of your potential rental accommodation to see what your neighbours look like and what their daily routine consists of.

Today's digital investigative efforts are driven by an overwhelming desire not to be bested. An Irish woman lives in perpetual fear that someone out there GOT A BETTER DEAL than her. This is a side effect of her fiercely competitive nature as alluded to in previous chapters. There is always the horrific possibility that she could have found a larger apartment with a nicer pool or a cheaper flight, and so the search continues *ad infinitum*. An amusing way to pass the time on a flight is to sit next to an Irish woman and engage her in friendly chit-chat. Then casually mention the fabulous deal you got by booking your flight at the last possible minute. Make sure the price you refer to is ridiculously low and watch the colour drain from her face. If you want to ruin her entire holiday, you could also mention the grandiose seven-bedroom villa you got for €100 a week due to a cancellation. She will be incapable of enjoying her holiday, devastated in the knowledge that you are having a cheaper vacation than her – and in flashier accommodation. To add insult to injury, you pulled off this heist as a direct result of your slovenly behaviour, doing little or no research and booking everything at the very last minute.

⋏ Camel Toe ⋏

Then there is the task of purchasing holiday clothing. Every year an Irish woman will go out and buy exactly the same uniform of summer holiday clothes as if stuck in a retail version of *Groundhog Day*. The annual purchases consist of the following:

* a couple of full-length, flowery sundresses;

* a pair of unflattering, knee-length khaki shorts; and

* the obligatory pair of white trousers.

All Irish women have a flawed mental picture of themselves looking sexy and sophisticated in a pair of white trousers. The sad fact is that Irish women cannot wear white trousers as they are unable to desist from the incessant feeding of people and the constant cleaning of things. Their milky trews will be mud-streaked and food-stained in seconds flat. White trousers have a predilection for VPL, and so should really never be worn anyway. Visible Panty Lines are bad enough, but if the trousers are on the tight side you could be dealing with an outbreak of Camel Toe.

There's a thin line (no pun intended) between figure-hugging and Camel Toe. Once an Irish girl has been spotted sporting an obvious case of Camel Toe, it is all anyone will *ever* remember about her. Perhaps she will develop a cure for cancer or receive the Nobel Peace Prize for the part she plays in the Middle Eastern ceasefire. It doesn't matter; she will be Missy Tight Pants Camel Toe for the rest of her mortal days.

The aforementioned summer clothes are purchased, worn during one holiday, then carefully packed away and never seen again. There is a black hole or void in all houses where the infinite space is rendered finite due to a glut of summer clothes, telescopes and smoothie makers, otherwise known as the Aldi Abyss.

⋏ The Supermercado ⋏

Upon arrival at her holiday destination, an Irish woman will be unable to get into holiday mode until she has stocked up. She races off to the nearest supermarket and purchases enough food and household items to run a small hotel for the entire summer season. This includes a large selection of liquor that she wouldn't dream of buying at home, but sure it's so cheap they're practically giving the Malibu away. When she is in line at the checkout she will make a mental note of the price of every purchase so she can impress people when she gets back to Ireland. She considers herself to be somehow responsible and assumes all credit for the ridiculously low cost of items in her local *supermercado*. It also means she can entertain herself and annoy all her colleagues by forcing them to guess how much two weeks' worth of food and drink shopping cost her on the trip. This is marginally less tedious than being forced to look at her 300+ holiday photos.

⋌ Camel Ride ⋋

The day-to-day activities in which an Irish woman engages on vacation is an exhausting cycle of drinking, shopping, going to and from the beach, and constant eating. The big plus for an Irish woman is that she is thousands of miles away from anyone who knows her. This anonymity and new-found freedom opens up a world of opportunities. It is interesting to note that once an Irish woman escapes from the social confines of her home country and the watchful eyes of her neighbours, the first thing that she does is to squeeze into her white pants, head to the nearest Irish bar and do the Macarena.

The following 'couldn't give two fucks' behaviour that an Irish woman adopts while on holidays is antithetical to her typical conduct on Irish soil. She:

* Commences her alcohol consumption immediately after her continental, sausage-free breakfast and continues to drink all day and all night;

* Replaces her fail-safe pint of lager with exotic cocktails festooned with gaudy fruit and alarming sparklers;

* Keeps her children in restaurants until 10 o'clock at night and allows them to run riot, tormenting staff and fellow diners alike;

* Straps inflatable rings and flotation devices to every inch of her children's bodies so that she can nod off beside the pool;

* Does not do the washing-up in the holiday apartment and leaves damp, sand-filled clothing lying all over the floor;

* Lives in harmony with the local cockroaches and geckos without feeling compelled to bludgeon them to death and hoover them up;

* Exposes inordinate amounts of flesh until her nipples get badly sunburnt – still, at least the travel insurance didn't go to waste;

* Exposes inordinate amounts of flesh so that her arse causes corneal flash burns and temporary blindness amongst her fellow sunbathers;

* Partakes in paragliding, scuba diving or a camel ride with a panty-liner firmly in place;

* Is openly friendly to foreigners and genuinely interested in their culture and traditions;

* Speaks English slowly for the first and only time in her life, but with a generic foreign accent designed to make it comprehensible to the non-English-speaking natives;

* Flirts outrageously with shiny, lecherous waiters;

* Tips the shiny, lecherous waiters;

* Belly dances with the shiny, lecherous waiters;

* Writes her postcards on the very last night of her holiday and posts them on the way to the airport because she just couldn't give two fucks.

⚡ Holiday Friendships ⚡

Being a ridiculously over-friendly person, she will make at least five new friends on holiday. The friendships are always with fellow Irish holidaymakers and are usually instigated by the communal sharing of inflatable swimming pool accessories on day two of the stay. On day three, the friendship is further cemented by comparing degrees of sunburn, quantities of mosquito bites and prices of accommodation (see earlier section on Holiday Deals). By day four, an Irish woman will have booked all the same day trips as her new-found friends and they will meet up for dinner and a feed of drink every night for the remainder of the vacation. She firmly believes they will be bosom buddies for the rest of their lives. The only downside to this social triumph is the risk that her new besties will post photos of the belly dancing/camel ride on Facebook. She insists on all her fellow holidaymakers being bound to secrecy about these diversions by engaging them in a Costa Del Covenant. No one must ever breathe a word or post a picture on any form of social media, on pain of death. As the holiday draws to a close, so great is her sorrow at parting from her new soulmates that she may even shed a tear when the time comes to say goodbye. An Irish woman will ensure that she gets all their contact details and solemnly swears that she will drive to Louth/Navan (delete as appropriate) to visit them as soon as she can.

However, by the time she has settled into her seat on the plane she will already have begun the inevitable character assassination. She will reflect on the fact that her new friends were a bit tight with their Lira and weren't exactly rushing up to the bar to get the cocktails in. On further reflection, she determines that one of them had a really loud annoying laugh and another one ruined her chillaxing time by the pool by recounting tedious stories about how much she hates her manager at work. Truth be told, she really had very little in common with them. By the time the 'fasten your seatbelt' sign has come on she has unfriended them on Facebook, deleted their numbers from her phone and can no longer remember their names or what they looked like.

Upon setting foot on Irish soil, she is seized by paroxysms of shame about her reckless abandonment while on her hols. She will feel the need to partake in some self-castigation in the form of penance the very day of her return. Defrosting the freezer or whisking her mother off to the Stations of the Cross will achieve the requisite absolution. No matter how successful the holiday was, an Irish woman will always be secretly glad to return home. Irrespective of the fact that she is arriving back to a country in the midst of torrential rain and financial ruin, she will relish drinking a decent cup of tea and catching up with her friends and family.

10.
Irish Women

A User's Manual

By now the reader should have gained some valuable insight into this engaging and complex creature, but how should you approach such a woman? What is the best way to handle these fractious females? Whether your contact with her is due to a social engagement or of the more professional variety, it is important to tread carefully. Many men have made the mistake of underestimating an Irish woman, but not many have lived to tell the tale. You may be pleasantly surprised and find yourself in the company of a sweet-natured matriarch, but it's best to prepare yourself for more of a sheela-na-gig type of gal. The following Do's and Don'ts section proffers advice on how best to behave when interacting with an Irish woman.

Don't underestimate her intelligence: Whether they have benefitted from a lengthy education or not, most Irish women are smart, and you rarely meet a slow-witted Irish woman. We have plenty of bitches, gossips and martyrs, but halfwits are noticeable in their absence. Never underestimate the intellectual powers of an Irish woman. Even if she gives the overall impression of being innocent and naïve, or looks like someone who was quite possibly reared by wolves, the chances are she will be shrewd, hyper-aware and an excellent judge of character. All it takes is a couple of furtive sniffs and she will have your measure. And, most importantly, there is no point in trying to pretend to be something you're not, as all Irish women have an innate bullshit-detection mechanism.

Do introduce a sad story into the conversation: She is quick to take offence and will often go out of her way to identify slights or perceived insults. If you happen to be from England, you will need to go that extra mile to convince her that you are not treating her like an illiterate peasant. Should you unwittingly insult an Irish woman, remember: you can be exonerated with the introduction of a heartbreaking story. Immediately recounting an unfortunate series of events in your life should get you over your initial transgression. If you are ever at a loss for a sorrowful story, you can default to 'Talk to Joe' tactics. Irish women are fascinated by scams, stories about people who were adopted and urban myths. Some old reliables include con men pretending to be roofers who rip off old ladies and people who were born in Ireland to single mothers, adopted abroad and are currently searching for their elusive Irish Mammy. More recent additions feature Italians selling fake leather jackets, phone calls from fraudulent technical support personnel and people that develop a large spot on their arm that eventually erupts with baby spiders. The introduction of any of the aforementioned subjects will ensure a rapt audience.

Do offer her an alcoholic beverage, no matter what the occasion: You may be her blind date, her gynaecologist or the person she has just rear-ended, it matters not. The offer of a swift one is always a welcome one. You do not want to be perceived to be tight with money at the bar, so at the very least you must attempt to pay for everything. She will never actually let you and will always insist on paying her way, but will be furious if you don't offer.

Don't overdo it: Like most complex social norms, there is a thin line between being generous and flashing your cash or showing off. Try not to step over this imaginary line or you will swiftly plummet from hero to zero.

Do make her laugh: It is extremely important to be good craic, and the introduction of the word 'fuck' or 'shite' should be viewed as the ultimate ice-breaker.

Don't overdo it: Don't go overboard on the swearing or the hilarity as you don't want to come across as a fuckin' eejit. Use her level of profanity as a guideline. Being talkative is a plus, but the Irish woman should drive most of the conversation. Reciting lengthy, detailed descriptions about any topic is a no-no. She is FAR TOO BUSY to stand around listening to you all day; your speech should be of the sound-bite variety. Should you find, at any given point, that her eyes are starting to glaze over, introduce the topic of a recent holiday. Recounting how you paid far too much for your flights and accommodation should bring you back from the brink.

Do praise her children: If she is a Mammy, you must remember the names and ages of her children and ask how they are doing. She will immediately make some disparaging remark about them. This is dangerous territory. On no account should you agree with her (see Chapter 8). You must immediately wax lyrical about their stunning good looks and obvious genius, and then subtly change the subject.

Don't pay her a compliment: Having played a blinder on the topic of her offspring, you should not be tempted to overreach yourself by complimenting the Irish woman herself. This is a social faux pas from which you will never recover. Any reference to her good looks or fabulous outfit will raise her hackles and you will thereafter be viewed with complete contempt.

Don't be concerned if she doesn't come back from the toilet: If you find yourself out on a date with an Irish girl, at some point during the night she may disappear off to the toilet for an hour or so – in fact, she may never come back. You should not overreact; this is perfectly normal behaviour for an Irish lass on a night out. There are a couple of simple explanations for this vanishing act:

1. She has bumped into someone in the bathroom that she used to work/go to school with and they are having a catch-up on everything that has happened to them during the intervening decade. She will be completely oblivious to

your discomfort and will immediately write you off as being 'no craic' should you admonish her on her return.

2. She has collapsed in an alcoholic stupor on the floor of the cubicle in the toilet. Due to the fact that most Irish girls will have had a few stiff ones during the Prinks session, it is highly likely that she will be well tanked up in advance of meeting you. If you add the couple of rounds of Jägerbombs she insisted you both drink to take the edge off her date night nerves, she may in fact be completely hammered by the time she excuses herself to go powder her nose. You may notice a couple of bouncers running through the bar and a small crowd gathering outside the ladies' bathroom while the security personnel try to break down the cubicle door. Your date is the person flaked out on the other side of the door, oblivious to the entire goings-on, which is ironic, as it would have made her night to witness all the drama. Don't be too shocked if she contacts you the next day to have a giggle about the 'savage craic' that you had and suggests that you do it again sometime.

3. She has had a group IM session with her buddies in the toilet during which she has recounted

what you are wearing and everything that you have said to her so far. Every word has been scrutinised for hidden meaning and an in-depth analysis of your body language has been carried out. You have been tried and convicted, and unfortunately your date's buddies have found you unworthy. Subsequently, the Irish lass has escaped from the ladies' bathroom by dragging the sanitary disposal bin over to the window, hoisting herself up and climbing out head first – all because you had the audacity to suggest that *Made in Chelsea* is actually a crock of shite.

Do not make fun of the Catholic Church: Many Irish women feel the need to play down their beliefs and any religious practices they engage in for fear of being ridiculed by their peers. This has resulted in a phenomenon known as Closet Catholicism. To be on the safe side, you should desist from blasphemy and limit any references to paedophile priests and Bishop Eamon Casey's progeny. If on a Saturday night out you are lucky enough to hook up with an Irish girl and have a crazy night of debauchery with said Irish babe, don't be surprised if she magically transforms into a practising Catholic on the stroke of half past ten the following morning. By and large, most Irish women will limit their religious practices to the bare minimum requirements, such as only attending Mass on the day of a wedding, funeral, Holy Communion, Confirmation or a Baptism, thereby earning themselves the dubious title of Sacrament Whores. Should some disaster befall them, or they know someone who is taking the driving test/sitting important exams, they may also partake in the low maintenance ritualistic practice of lighting a candle. Finally, never slag off St Anthony as he has been known to pull out all the stops for even the most lapsed Catholic.

Do use the following Irish Bitchspeak translator as a guide to what an Irish woman is really saying to you:
When an Irish woman says: 'Sorry.'
What she means: 'Excuse me,' or 'Get out of my way'.
When an Irish woman says: 'Sorry?'
What she means: 'I cannot believe you had the nerve to just say that.'
What she doesn't mean: 'Sorry.'

When an Irish woman says: 'Fuck off!'
What she means: 'No way, are you serious? That's shockin' news.'

When an Irish woman says: 'Fuck off!' (accompanied by laughter)
What she means: 'I acknowledge that you are flirting with me and I am reciprocating that flirtation.'
What she doesn't mean: 'Go away.'

When an Irish woman says: 'How's it going? How're ya doing? How're things?'
What she means: 'Hi.'
What she doesn't mean: 'How's it going? How're ya doing? How're things?'

When an Irish woman says: 'It's fine.'
What she means: 'It has never been fine for one millisecond and you are in a world of trouble.'
What she doesn't mean: 'I don't mind.'

When an Irish woman says: 'Ah, sure you're a gas man.'
What she means: 'You're a pain in the hole.'
What she doesn't mean: 'I find you terribly amusing.'

When an Irish woman says: 'Wait till I tell ya' or 'GUESS WHAT!'
What she means: 'I have the juiciest, toe-curling, scandalous gossip to impart.'

What she doesn't mean: 'I have something to tell you but will delay until a later date.'

Note: *when an Irish woman hears a fellow Irish woman saying 'Wait till I tell ya' she will crash cars, sink ships and abandon loved ones to ensure she is privy to the next sentence that is uttered.*

When an Irish woman talking on the phone says: 'Bye, Bye, Bye, Bye, Bye, Bye, Bye.........Bye.'
What she means: 'I am the Busiest Woman in Ireland.'
What she doesn't mean: 'Goodbye.'

*

No matter how much sage advice you receive, you will never fully understand the enigmatic Irish woman. The day may come when you feel that you have begun to comprehend what drives and inspires these women and, more importantly, how not to piss them off, but this self-congratulation will be all too brief as an Irish woman is full of surprises. At any given moment she will announce that she has decided to emigrate, go back to college or take up basket weaving. So it's best not to get too complacent, just hold tight and enjoy the ride (in the traditional sense of the word).

Conclusion

Over ten chapters we have learned a lot about the Irish woman, past and present, but what conclusion can we reach about the upshot of these combined psychological, environmental and sociological influences? On the surface, an Irish woman may exhibit all the stereotypical characteristics associated with her gender and nationality: she is friendly, hard-working and superstitious. However, you don't have to dig too hard to discover a plethora of deeply ingrained psychological issues. Are these the consequence of spending their formative years in the company of nuns? Do the combined effects of Catholic guilt, heavy drinking and sewing class produce a definitive type of girl? I would argue that they do.

Irish women are clearly great craic, and although they are obsessed with death they don't take life too seriously. Maybe the fear of tragic accidents or contracting Cancer has encouraged them to exist in the moment and live each day as if it's their last. Equally, our FOMO is extreme, and having been lumbered with the 'heavy drinkers' tag we seem determined to live up to this reputation, irrespective of how clichéd and ill-advised it is.

Our sense of humour is a strange combination of sharp, caustic wit and self-deprecation. The self-deprecation stems from our traditionally low self-esteem; we are very aware of our foibles and will laugh heartily at ourselves. We will slag everyone unmercifully – nobody is exempt – but it's hard to be offended as we are just as quick to take the piss out of ourselves. This unfailing good humour and desire to maintain a savage level of craic has a manic intensity that is verging on hysteria, and belies yet further psychosis. Once the hilarity stops and the laughter has been silenced, an Irish woman will be left with nothing but her own thoughts, worries and resentments. She may have to accept some home truths: that her children are just average and without any discernible talents, that the marble tiles in her bathroom weren't worth an extra five years on her mortgage and that the Irish soccer team may never again qualify for the World Cup. Once she shakes herself out of this depressing reverie, she will be back to full-blown slagging, knee-slapping and unfailing good humour.

Irish Bitches Be Crazy has also provided a chronological account of Irish beauty techniques through the ages and has examined the awkward progression of Irish women from Extreme Virginism to present-day Sluttishness. Through this analysis we see how increased secularisation and globalisation has freed up your average Irish gal by providing her with infinitely more freedom and choices, transforming her into a significantly more self-assured individual. Some practices never change though, and an Irish woman's funeral etiquette and questionable holiday behaviour remain steadfast.

In order to avoid shameless generalisation regarding the craziness, or lack thereof, of the female population of Ireland, I have attempted to categorise the different types of Irish women in existence today. By undertaking the following quiz you can identify what type of Irish woman you are and how high you score in the lunacy spectrum.

What kind of Irish woman are you?

1. You have just won the lottery. Do you:
    a)   Immediately ditch your hipster look and spend thousands on designer tracksuits, get some butt implants and a full-time brow trainer and move to LA?

b) Leave the winning ticket in a drawer for a month, petrified that you'll get no luck from it, then change your mind and cash it in once you realise you have a Holy Communion and a Confirmation on this year?

c) Build a massive house right behind your existing house, cut down all the trees in the area so you can tarmac every square inch of the surrounding land and send your children to Swiss finishing school to take the scanger/ redneck edge off them (delete as appropriate based on urban or rural location)?

2. The guy or girl you have been lusting after for ages is walking past you when all of a sudden they stop and start conversing with you. Do you:

a) Ignore them, they're obviously a complete loser as no one hooks up organically these days?

b) Speak to them with your eyes averted in hushed, reverential tones as you don't want to interrupt the Prayers of the Faithful?

c) Grab them by the forearm and start babbling nervously with increasing levels of volume, eventually listing off the price of houses in the area and roaring the details of what you had for breakfast that morning into their startled face?

3. You are in the canteen at work having a good ol' bitch about someone you know when your boss over-hears you. Your boss then informs you that the person you are gossiping about is their first cousin. Do you:

a) Immediately start apologising in breathless girly speak, punctuated with 'OMG's and 'I am sooooo, like, sorry'? Then take a selfie of your bright red, freaked-out head beside your boss's furious head and race back to your desk to post it on Snapchat?

b) Smile sweetly and say, 'you must have misheard me, it was *utter completely different name* I was talking about and not your first cousin'? After all, you are a consummate professional in the realm of gossiping and can take this kind of thing in your stride.

c) Set off the fire alarm to create a diversion, thus giving yourself a chance to leave the office undetected, jump into your car and drive like a maniac to the nearest recruitment agency office?

4. You are on a first date in a nice restaurant when you notice that your date has a pubic hair stuck in between their front teeth. Do you:

a) Casually enquire if it belongs to a male or female sexual partner because you are cool with that kinda thing, then suggest that the three of you get together, your philosophy being 'don't knock it till you try it'?

b) Stand up, point your finger at them and dramatically accuse them of engaging in the sinful practice of Lust of the Muff? Then call for the cheque and insist on paying while repeatedly apologising to the staff and the other diners for causing a scene.

c) Accidentally-on-purpose fling your glass of wine into their lap so that they have to go to the bathroom to get cleaned up? Once they're out of sight, grab your bag, drop on all fours and commando roll out of the restaurant.

5. If you were a movie what movie would you be?

a) *The Social Network*
b) *Misery*
c) *Bridesmaids*

Answers

If you chose mostly (a)'s then…

… you are a younger Irish girl with mid-level scoring on the lunacy spectrum. As you were not educated by nuns, your generation are capable of enjoying themselves without feeling condemned to the depths of hell for their actions. You are far more sexually open and can have a one-night stand without having to engage in self-flagellation and climb Croagh Patrick the following morning. Although you are exempt from some of the more traditional lunacy of your Irish female ancestry, and are quite capable of graciously accepting a compliment, you have simply replaced some of their quainter, old-fashioned psychoses with some shiny new madness. Your addiction to social networking and alienation from the tangible world around you is bordering on Japanese levels. You are constantly engaged in an uphill battle to be quirky and original in your style and habits, as everything has already been done, at least twice. No sooner have you dressed yourself in a shapeless floral housecoat, draped a woollen shawl over your shoulders and headed off on your unicycle smoking a pipe, than all of a sudden your personal style has become mainstream and the *Peig power* look is trending in Norway.

If you chose mostly (b)'s then...
... you are an older and more traditional Irish lady. You have not fallen prey to the scourge of secularism and have a vague notion that twerking has something to do with robots taking peoples jobs. At first glance,

you appear to be quite sane and less flaky than your younger counterparts. You have strong religious convictions and an unwavering belief in the evils of sex before marriage. You didn't get caught up in the mania of the Celtic Tiger, preferring to squirrel away your spare change in your knickers drawer – a rainy day being a foregone conclusion in this country. You are quick to remind your more *flathúlach*/extravagant friends that it isn't that long since Irish women were so impoverished they had to walk to school and eat grass for dinner. Nonetheless, beneath this self-contained and stoic exterior lies a deeply superstitious and oft-times irrational mindset. As well as the conventional Catholic catechism, you also firmly believe in:

* Fairies stealing boy babies and replacing them with changelings;

* The bad karma associated with walking over gravestones – especially if the family who own the grave are nearby and armed with machetes;

* If you eat too much butter, you get a ring around your heart and you die;

* An itchy hand means you are going to come into money, an itchy nose means you are going to have

a fight with someone. Itchy anywhere else is most likely a hygiene issue;

* Eradicating bad luck by waving at magpies and throwing salt over your shoulder;

* If you swallow chewing gum your insides stick together and you die; and

* The ownership of a four-leaf clover negates all of the above, but is utterly worthless on Friday 13th.

As the world at large is full of these potential traps and pitfalls, it means that you have to be constantly on your guard and are inherently wary. Your demeanour may be friendly but you are cagey and suspicious by nature. The long list of things you don't trust includes: bankers, hippies, cats, computers, motivational speakers, bikers, Met Éireann, men, insurance companies, high-rise car parks and foxes. You have an irrational fear of spiders, mice and foreigners.

If you chose mostly (c)'s then…
… you are an Irish woman in the 30+ age group. You score quite high on the lunacy spectrum due to carrying around most of the archaic derangement of your grandmother's generation, as well as

adopting a touch of the more modern insanity of the younger Irish female. As a non-practising Catholic or Sacrament Whore, you want to have your host and eat it. You don't actually want to spend time on your religion, preferring to roll it out during life's more troublesome moments, like a cheap insurance policy, with God as the provider and your parish priest acting as broker. Equally, you are trying to be free-spirited and liberated, imagining yourself and your friends to be like the Irish version of *Sex and the City*. However, your Irish Catholic programming keeps reverting to default shame mode. This contradiction is having a huge strain on your mental health. Similarly, having sailed through the Boom in Ireland, you grew accustomed to expensive holidays, Pandora bracelets and four-wheel drives. You are now feeling quite peevish about struggling through the aftermath; the austerity plan hasn't quite kicked in yet and the bills are mounting. You distract yourself by dashing from work to the school gates with a manic schedule that includes wedding receptions, funeral parlours and fundraising table quizzes. Your life is hectic, your kids are spoiled rotten and your nights out are increasingly drunken and rampageous. If your life were a scene in a Scorsese gangster movie, you'd be on the verge of the climactic police raid, the epic build-up music would be getting louder and in five minutes' time the helicopters would be swooping in full of FBI officers, hell-bent on putting an end to all the madness.

*

Conclusively, whether an Irish woman is young or old, dealing with school gate protocol or engaged in the Walk of Shame, they may be slightly unhinged, but equally they are generous and kind. Irish women have a very important quality: the knack of making people feel good about themselves. They are genuinely interested in you … especially if you have recently transferred funds to the Prince of Nigeria having been promised an influx of West African riches in a personalised letter from him. So although Irish Bitches may in fact be quite Crazy, having one of these unique women in your life is ultimately a very rewarding and worthwhile experience.

Acknowledgements

I would like to thank the following people: Conor 'Monty' Montague for wading through first drafts and giving me excellent editing advice. Without Monty's support, *Irish Bitches Be Crazy* would never have been written. Fellow writers Sheila Bugler and Charlie Adley for their words of wisdom. Mad Mary Finnerty for her *cailleach* know-how and Stephen O'Cualain's Irish translations of same. Sarah 'Vintage Venom' Magliocco for her brilliant insights into the iPhone generation and Ray Kelly for knowing what's funny and what's not. Stephen, Vera and Lorraine for replying to endless, lengthy emails. Dan Bolger and all at New Island for believing in the book. Special thanks to the gang of Irish women that I am lucky to have as my friends and whose lunacy inspired this book, you know who you are. My parents Henry and Deirdre for all their support and literary leanings. Finally, my 'lads' Patsy, Paddy and Rían who are my world but more importantly who put up with me both during the writing of this book and on a daily basis.